©

**Copyright 2022 - All rights reserved.**

You may not reproduce, duplicate or send the contents of this book without direct written permission from the author. You cannot apply hereby despite any circumstance blame the publisher or hold him or her to legal responsibility for any reparation, compensations, or monetary forfeiture owing to the information included herein, either in a direct or an indirect way.

Legal Notice: This book has copyright protection. You can use the book for personal purposes. You should not sell, use, alter, distribute, quote, take excerpts, or paraphrase in part or whole the material contained in this book without obtaining the permission of the author first.

Disclaimer Notice: You must take note that the information in this document is for casual reading and entertainment purposes only. We have made every attempt to provide accurate, up-to-date, and reliable information. We do not express or imply guarantees of any kind. The persons who read admit that the writer is not occupied in giving legal, financial, medical, or other advice. We put this book content by sourcing various places.

Please consult a licensed professional before you try any techniques shown in this book. By going through this document, the book lover comes to an an agreement that under no situation is the author accountable for any forfeiture, direct or indirect, which they may incur because of the use of material contained in this document, including, but not limited to, — errors, omissions, or inaccuracies.

# Weight Lifting
## Log Book

**Belongs to**

_____
_____

**Date:** _____  **Muscle Group:** _____

S  M  T  W  T  F  S    **Start Time** _____
○  ○  ○  ○  ○  ○  ○

**Weight:** _____    **Finish Time** _____

☐ **Upper Body**    ☐ **Lower Body**    ☐ **Abs**

| Exercise | Set | 1 | 2 | 3 | 4 | 5 | 6 | 7 |
|---|---|---|---|---|---|---|---|---|
|  | Reps |  |  |  |  |  |  |  |
|  | Weight |  |  |  |  |  |  |  |
|  | Reps |  |  |  |  |  |  |  |
|  | Weight |  |  |  |  |  |  |  |
|  | Reps |  |  |  |  |  |  |  |
|  | Weight |  |  |  |  |  |  |  |
|  | Reps |  |  |  |  |  |  |  |
|  | Weight |  |  |  |  |  |  |  |
|  | Reps |  |  |  |  |  |  |  |
|  | Weight |  |  |  |  |  |  |  |
|  | Reps |  |  |  |  |  |  |  |
|  | Weight |  |  |  |  |  |  |  |
|  | Reps |  |  |  |  |  |  |  |
|  | Weight |  |  |  |  |  |  |  |
|  | Reps |  |  |  |  |  |  |  |
|  | Weight |  |  |  |  |  |  |  |

| Cardio | Time | Distance | Heart Rate | Cals Burned |
|---|---|---|---|---|
|  |  |  |  |  |
|  |  |  |  |  |
|  |  |  |  |  |

### Measurements

| Neck | R Bicep | L Bicep | Chest | Waist | Hips | R Thigh | L Thigh | Calf |
|---|---|---|---|---|---|---|---|---|
|  |  |  |  |  |  |  |  |  |
|  |  |  |  |  |  |  |  |  |
|  |  |  |  |  |  |  |  |  |

**Date:** _____  **Muscle Group:** _____

S  M  T  W  T  F  S   **Start Time** _____
○  ○  ○  ○  ○  ○  ○

**Weight:** _____  **Finish Time** _____

☐ **Upper Body**   ☐ **Lower Body**   ☐ **Abs**

| Exercise | Set | 1 | 2 | 3 | 4 | 5 | 6 | 7 |
|---|---|---|---|---|---|---|---|---|
|  | Reps |  |  |  |  |  |  |  |
|  | Weight |  |  |  |  |  |  |  |
|  | Reps |  |  |  |  |  |  |  |
|  | Weight |  |  |  |  |  |  |  |
|  | Reps |  |  |  |  |  |  |  |
|  | Weight |  |  |  |  |  |  |  |
|  | Reps |  |  |  |  |  |  |  |
|  | Weight |  |  |  |  |  |  |  |
|  | Reps |  |  |  |  |  |  |  |
|  | Weight |  |  |  |  |  |  |  |
|  | Reps |  |  |  |  |  |  |  |
|  | Weight |  |  |  |  |  |  |  |
|  | Reps |  |  |  |  |  |  |  |
|  | Weight |  |  |  |  |  |  |  |
|  | Reps |  |  |  |  |  |  |  |
|  | Weight |  |  |  |  |  |  |  |

| Cardio | Time | Distance | Heart Rate | Cals Burned |
|---|---|---|---|---|
|  |  |  |  |  |
|  |  |  |  |  |
|  |  |  |  |  |

## Measurements

| Neck | R Bicep | L Bicep | Chest | Waist | Hips | R Thigh | L Thigh | Calf |
|---|---|---|---|---|---|---|---|---|
|  |  |  |  |  |  |  |  |  |
|  |  |  |  |  |  |  |  |  |
|  |  |  |  |  |  |  |  |  |

**Date:** _____  **Muscle Group:** _____

S  M  T  W  T  F  S   **Start Time** _____
○  ○  ○  ○  ○  ○  ○

**Weight:** _____  **Finish Time** _____

☐ Upper Body    ☐ Lower Body    ☐ Abs

| Exercise | Set | 1 | 2 | 3 | 4 | 5 | 6 | 7 |
|---|---|---|---|---|---|---|---|---|
|  | Reps |  |  |  |  |  |  |  |
|  | Weight |  |  |  |  |  |  |  |
|  | Reps |  |  |  |  |  |  |  |
|  | Weight |  |  |  |  |  |  |  |
|  | Reps |  |  |  |  |  |  |  |
|  | Weight |  |  |  |  |  |  |  |
|  | Reps |  |  |  |  |  |  |  |
|  | Weight |  |  |  |  |  |  |  |
|  | Reps |  |  |  |  |  |  |  |
|  | Weight |  |  |  |  |  |  |  |
|  | Reps |  |  |  |  |  |  |  |
|  | Weight |  |  |  |  |  |  |  |
|  | Reps |  |  |  |  |  |  |  |
|  | Weight |  |  |  |  |  |  |  |
|  | Reps |  |  |  |  |  |  |  |
|  | Weight |  |  |  |  |  |  |  |

| Cardio | Time | Distance | Heart Rate | Cals Burned |
|---|---|---|---|---|
|  |  |  |  |  |
|  |  |  |  |  |
|  |  |  |  |  |

### Measurements

| Neck | R Bicep | L Bicep | Chest | Waist | Hips | R Thigh | L Thigh | Calf |
|---|---|---|---|---|---|---|---|---|
|  |  |  |  |  |  |  |  |  |
|  |  |  |  |  |  |  |  |  |
|  |  |  |  |  |  |  |  |  |

Date: _____  Muscle Group: _____

S M T W T F S  Start Time _____
○ ○ ○ ○ ○ ○ ○

Weight: _____  Finish Time _____

☐ Upper Body  ☐ Lower Body  ☐ Abs

| Exercise | Set | 1 | 2 | 3 | 4 | 5 | 6 | 7 |
|---|---|---|---|---|---|---|---|---|
|  | Reps |  |  |  |  |  |  |  |
|  | Weight |  |  |  |  |  |  |  |
|  | Reps |  |  |  |  |  |  |  |
|  | Weight |  |  |  |  |  |  |  |
|  | Reps |  |  |  |  |  |  |  |
|  | Weight |  |  |  |  |  |  |  |
|  | Reps |  |  |  |  |  |  |  |
|  | Weight |  |  |  |  |  |  |  |
|  | Reps |  |  |  |  |  |  |  |
|  | Weight |  |  |  |  |  |  |  |
|  | Reps |  |  |  |  |  |  |  |
|  | Weight |  |  |  |  |  |  |  |
|  | Reps |  |  |  |  |  |  |  |
|  | Weight |  |  |  |  |  |  |  |
|  | Reps |  |  |  |  |  |  |  |
|  | Weight |  |  |  |  |  |  |  |

| Cardio | Time | Distance | Heart Rate | Cals Burned |
|---|---|---|---|---|
|  |  |  |  |  |
|  |  |  |  |  |
|  |  |  |  |  |

## Measurements

| Neck | R Bicep | L Bicep | Chest | Waist | Hips | R Thigh | L Thigh | Calf |
|---|---|---|---|---|---|---|---|---|
|  |  |  |  |  |  |  |  |  |
|  |  |  |  |  |  |  |  |  |
|  |  |  |  |  |  |  |  |  |

**Date:** _____ **Muscle Group:** _____

S M T W T F S **Start Time** _____
○ ○ ○ ○ ○ ○ ○

**Weight:** _____ **Finish Time** _____

☐ Upper Body  ☐ Lower Body  ☐ Abs

| Exercise | Set | 1 | 2 | 3 | 4 | 5 | 6 | 7 |
|---|---|---|---|---|---|---|---|---|
|  | Reps |  |  |  |  |  |  |  |
|  | Weight |  |  |  |  |  |  |  |
|  | Reps |  |  |  |  |  |  |  |
|  | Weight |  |  |  |  |  |  |  |
|  | Reps |  |  |  |  |  |  |  |
|  | Weight |  |  |  |  |  |  |  |
|  | Reps |  |  |  |  |  |  |  |
|  | Weight |  |  |  |  |  |  |  |
|  | Reps |  |  |  |  |  |  |  |
|  | Weight |  |  |  |  |  |  |  |
|  | Reps |  |  |  |  |  |  |  |
|  | Weight |  |  |  |  |  |  |  |
|  | Reps |  |  |  |  |  |  |  |
|  | Weight |  |  |  |  |  |  |  |
|  | Reps |  |  |  |  |  |  |  |
|  | Weight |  |  |  |  |  |  |  |

| Cardio | Time | Distance | Heart Rate | Cals Burned |
|---|---|---|---|---|
|  |  |  |  |  |
|  |  |  |  |  |
|  |  |  |  |  |

### Measurements

| Neck | R Bicep | L Bicep | Chest | Waist | Hips | R Thigh | L Thigh | Calf |
|---|---|---|---|---|---|---|---|---|
|  |  |  |  |  |  |  |  |  |
|  |  |  |  |  |  |  |  |  |
|  |  |  |  |  |  |  |  |  |

**Date:** _____  **Muscle Group:** _____

S  M  T  W  T  F  S     **Start Time** _____
○  ○  ○  ○  ○  ○  ○

**Weight:** _____  **Finish Time** _____

☐ **Upper Body**   ☐ **Lower Body**   ☐ **Abs**

| Exercise | Set | 1 | 2 | 3 | 4 | 5 | 6 | 7 |
|---|---|---|---|---|---|---|---|---|
|  | Reps |  |  |  |  |  |  |  |
|  | Weight |  |  |  |  |  |  |  |
|  | Reps |  |  |  |  |  |  |  |
|  | Weight |  |  |  |  |  |  |  |
|  | Reps |  |  |  |  |  |  |  |
|  | Weight |  |  |  |  |  |  |  |
|  | Reps |  |  |  |  |  |  |  |
|  | Weight |  |  |  |  |  |  |  |
|  | Reps |  |  |  |  |  |  |  |
|  | Weight |  |  |  |  |  |  |  |
|  | Reps |  |  |  |  |  |  |  |
|  | Weight |  |  |  |  |  |  |  |
|  | Reps |  |  |  |  |  |  |  |
|  | Weight |  |  |  |  |  |  |  |
|  | Reps |  |  |  |  |  |  |  |
|  | Weight |  |  |  |  |  |  |  |

| Cardio | Time | Distance | Heart Rate | Cals Burned |
|---|---|---|---|---|
|  |  |  |  |  |
|  |  |  |  |  |
|  |  |  |  |  |

## Measurements

| Neck | R Bicep | L Bicep | Chest | Waist | Hips | R Thigh | L Thigh | Calf |
|---|---|---|---|---|---|---|---|---|
|  |  |  |  |  |  |  |  |  |
|  |  |  |  |  |  |  |  |  |
|  |  |  |  |  |  |  |  |  |

Date: _____  Muscle Group: _____

S M T W T F S   Start Time _____
○ ○ ○ ○ ○ ○ ○

Weight: _____  Finish Time _____

☐ Upper Body  ☐ Lower Body  ☐ Abs

| Exercise | Set | 1 | 2 | 3 | 4 | 5 | 6 | 7 |
|---|---|---|---|---|---|---|---|---|
| | Reps | | | | | | | |
| | Weight | | | | | | | |
| | Reps | | | | | | | |
| | Weight | | | | | | | |
| | Reps | | | | | | | |
| | Weight | | | | | | | |
| | Reps | | | | | | | |
| | Weight | | | | | | | |
| | Reps | | | | | | | |
| | Weight | | | | | | | |
| | Reps | | | | | | | |
| | Weight | | | | | | | |
| | Reps | | | | | | | |
| | Weight | | | | | | | |
| | Reps | | | | | | | |
| | Weight | | | | | | | |

| Cardio | Time | Distance | Heart Rate | Cals Burned |
|---|---|---|---|---|
| | | | | |
| | | | | |
| | | | | |

## Measurements

| Neck | R Bicep | L Bicep | Chest | Waist | Hips | R Thigh | L Thigh | Calf |
|---|---|---|---|---|---|---|---|---|
| | | | | | | | | |
| | | | | | | | | |
| | | | | | | | | |

**Date:** _____  **Muscle Group:** _____

S  M  T  W  T  F  S
◯  ◯  ◯  ◯  ◯  ◯  ◯

**Start Time** _____

**Weight:** _____   **Finish Time** _____

☐ Upper Body     ☐ Lower Body     ☐ Abs

| Exercise | Set | 1 | 2 | 3 | 4 | 5 | 6 | 7 |
|---|---|---|---|---|---|---|---|---|
|  | Reps |  |  |  |  |  |  |  |
|  | Weight |  |  |  |  |  |  |  |
|  | Reps |  |  |  |  |  |  |  |
|  | Weight |  |  |  |  |  |  |  |
|  | Reps |  |  |  |  |  |  |  |
|  | Weight |  |  |  |  |  |  |  |
|  | Reps |  |  |  |  |  |  |  |
|  | Weight |  |  |  |  |  |  |  |
|  | Reps |  |  |  |  |  |  |  |
|  | Weight |  |  |  |  |  |  |  |
|  | Reps |  |  |  |  |  |  |  |
|  | Weight |  |  |  |  |  |  |  |
|  | Reps |  |  |  |  |  |  |  |
|  | Weight |  |  |  |  |  |  |  |
|  | Reps |  |  |  |  |  |  |  |
|  | Weight |  |  |  |  |  |  |  |

| Cardio | Time | Distance | Heart Rate | Cals Burned |
|---|---|---|---|---|
|  |  |  |  |  |
|  |  |  |  |  |
|  |  |  |  |  |

### Measurements

| Neck | R Bicep | L Bicep | Chest | Waist | Hips | R Thigh | L Thigh | Calf |
|---|---|---|---|---|---|---|---|---|
|  |  |  |  |  |  |  |  |  |
|  |  |  |  |  |  |  |  |  |
|  |  |  |  |  |  |  |  |  |

**Date:** _____  **Muscle Group:** _____

S  M  T  W  T  F  S   **Start Time** _____
○  ○  ○  ○  ○  ○  ○

**Weight:** _____  **Finish Time** _____

☐ Upper Body    ☐ Lower Body    ☐ Abs

| Exercise | Set | 1 | 2 | 3 | 4 | 5 | 6 | 7 |
|---|---|---|---|---|---|---|---|---|
|  | Reps |  |  |  |  |  |  |  |
|  | Weight |  |  |  |  |  |  |  |
|  | Reps |  |  |  |  |  |  |  |
|  | Weight |  |  |  |  |  |  |  |
|  | Reps |  |  |  |  |  |  |  |
|  | Weight |  |  |  |  |  |  |  |
|  | Reps |  |  |  |  |  |  |  |
|  | Weight |  |  |  |  |  |  |  |
|  | Reps |  |  |  |  |  |  |  |
|  | Weight |  |  |  |  |  |  |  |
|  | Reps |  |  |  |  |  |  |  |
|  | Weight |  |  |  |  |  |  |  |
|  | Reps |  |  |  |  |  |  |  |
|  | Weight |  |  |  |  |  |  |  |
|  | Reps |  |  |  |  |  |  |  |
|  | Weight |  |  |  |  |  |  |  |

| Cardio | Time | Distance | Heart Rate | Cals Burned |
|---|---|---|---|---|
|  |  |  |  |  |
|  |  |  |  |  |
|  |  |  |  |  |

### Measurements

| Neck | R Bicep | L Bicep | Chest | Waist | Hips | R Thigh | L Thigh | Calf |
|---|---|---|---|---|---|---|---|---|
|  |  |  |  |  |  |  |  |  |
|  |  |  |  |  |  |  |  |  |
|  |  |  |  |  |  |  |  |  |

**Date:** _____  **Muscle Group:** _____

S  M  T  W  T  F  S  **Start Time** _____
◯ ◯ ◯ ◯ ◯ ◯ ◯

**Weight:** _____  **Finish Time** _____

☐ **Upper Body**  ☐ **Lower Body**  ☐ **Abs**

| Exercise | Set | 1 | 2 | 3 | 4 | 5 | 6 | 7 |
|---|---|---|---|---|---|---|---|---|
|  | Reps |  |  |  |  |  |  |  |
|  | Weight |  |  |  |  |  |  |  |
|  | Reps |  |  |  |  |  |  |  |
|  | Weight |  |  |  |  |  |  |  |
|  | Reps |  |  |  |  |  |  |  |
|  | Weight |  |  |  |  |  |  |  |
|  | Reps |  |  |  |  |  |  |  |
|  | Weight |  |  |  |  |  |  |  |
|  | Reps |  |  |  |  |  |  |  |
|  | Weight |  |  |  |  |  |  |  |
|  | Reps |  |  |  |  |  |  |  |
|  | Weight |  |  |  |  |  |  |  |
|  | Reps |  |  |  |  |  |  |  |
|  | Weight |  |  |  |  |  |  |  |
|  | Reps |  |  |  |  |  |  |  |
|  | Weight |  |  |  |  |  |  |  |

| Cardio | Time | Distance | Heart Rate | Cals Burned |
|---|---|---|---|---|
|  |  |  |  |  |
|  |  |  |  |  |
|  |  |  |  |  |

### Measurements

| Neck | R Bicep | L Bicep | Chest | Waist | Hips | R Thigh | L Thigh | Calf |
|---|---|---|---|---|---|---|---|---|
|  |  |  |  |  |  |  |  |  |
|  |  |  |  |  |  |  |  |  |
|  |  |  |  |  |  |  |  |  |

Date: _____  Muscle Group: _____

S M T W T F S   Start Time _____
○ ○ ○ ○ ○ ○ ○

Weight: _____  Finish Time _____

☐ Upper Body    ☐ Lower Body    ☐ Abs

| Exercise | Set | 1 | 2 | 3 | 4 | 5 | 6 | 7 |
|---|---|---|---|---|---|---|---|---|
|  | Reps |  |  |  |  |  |  |  |
|  | Weight |  |  |  |  |  |  |  |
|  | Reps |  |  |  |  |  |  |  |
|  | Weight |  |  |  |  |  |  |  |
|  | Reps |  |  |  |  |  |  |  |
|  | Weight |  |  |  |  |  |  |  |
|  | Reps |  |  |  |  |  |  |  |
|  | Weight |  |  |  |  |  |  |  |
|  | Reps |  |  |  |  |  |  |  |
|  | Weight |  |  |  |  |  |  |  |
|  | Reps |  |  |  |  |  |  |  |
|  | Weight |  |  |  |  |  |  |  |
|  | Reps |  |  |  |  |  |  |  |
|  | Weight |  |  |  |  |  |  |  |
|  | Reps |  |  |  |  |  |  |  |
|  | Weight |  |  |  |  |  |  |  |

| Cardio | Time | Distance | Heart Rate | Cals Burned |
|---|---|---|---|---|
|  |  |  |  |  |
|  |  |  |  |  |
|  |  |  |  |  |

## Measurements

| Neck | R Bicep | L Bicep | Chest | Waist | Hips | R Thigh | L Thigh | Calf |
|---|---|---|---|---|---|---|---|---|
|  |  |  |  |  |  |  |  |  |
|  |  |  |  |  |  |  |  |  |
|  |  |  |  |  |  |  |  |  |

**Date:** _____ **Muscle Group:** _____

S  M  T  W  T  F  S
○  ○  ○  ○  ○  ○  ○     **Start Time** _____

**Weight:** _____ **Finish Time** _____

☐ **Upper Body**    ☐ **Lower Body**    ☐ **Abs**

| Exercise | Set | 1 | 2 | 3 | 4 | 5 | 6 | 7 |
|---|---|---|---|---|---|---|---|---|
|  | Reps |  |  |  |  |  |  |  |
|  | Weight |  |  |  |  |  |  |  |
|  | Reps |  |  |  |  |  |  |  |
|  | Weight |  |  |  |  |  |  |  |
|  | Reps |  |  |  |  |  |  |  |
|  | Weight |  |  |  |  |  |  |  |
|  | Reps |  |  |  |  |  |  |  |
|  | Weight |  |  |  |  |  |  |  |
|  | Reps |  |  |  |  |  |  |  |
|  | Weight |  |  |  |  |  |  |  |
|  | Reps |  |  |  |  |  |  |  |
|  | Weight |  |  |  |  |  |  |  |
|  | Reps |  |  |  |  |  |  |  |
|  | Weight |  |  |  |  |  |  |  |
|  | Reps |  |  |  |  |  |  |  |
|  | Weight |  |  |  |  |  |  |  |

| Cardio | Time | Distance | Heart Rate | Cals Burned |
|---|---|---|---|---|
|  |  |  |  |  |
|  |  |  |  |  |
|  |  |  |  |  |

### Measurements

| Neck | R Bicep | L Bicep | Chest | Waist | Hips | R Thigh | L Thigh | Calf |
|---|---|---|---|---|---|---|---|---|
|  |  |  |  |  |  |  |  |  |
|  |  |  |  |  |  |  |  |  |
|  |  |  |  |  |  |  |  |  |

**Date:** _____  **Muscle Group:** _____

S  M  T  W  T  F  S   **Start Time** _____
○  ○  ○  ○  ○  ○  ○

**Weight:** _____  **Finish Time** _____

☐ Upper Body    ☐ Lower Body    ☐ Abs

| Exercise | Set | 1 | 2 | 3 | 4 | 5 | 6 | 7 |
|---|---|---|---|---|---|---|---|---|
|  | Reps |  |  |  |  |  |  |  |
|  | Weight |  |  |  |  |  |  |  |
|  | Reps |  |  |  |  |  |  |  |
|  | Weight |  |  |  |  |  |  |  |
|  | Reps |  |  |  |  |  |  |  |
|  | Weight |  |  |  |  |  |  |  |
|  | Reps |  |  |  |  |  |  |  |
|  | Weight |  |  |  |  |  |  |  |
|  | Reps |  |  |  |  |  |  |  |
|  | Weight |  |  |  |  |  |  |  |
|  | Reps |  |  |  |  |  |  |  |
|  | Weight |  |  |  |  |  |  |  |
|  | Reps |  |  |  |  |  |  |  |
|  | Weight |  |  |  |  |  |  |  |
|  | Reps |  |  |  |  |  |  |  |
|  | Weight |  |  |  |  |  |  |  |

| Cardio | Time | Distance | Heart Rate | Cals Burned |
|---|---|---|---|---|
|  |  |  |  |  |
|  |  |  |  |  |
|  |  |  |  |  |

### Measurements

| Neck | R Bicep | L Bicep | Chest | Waist | Hips | R Thigh | L Thigh | Calf |
|---|---|---|---|---|---|---|---|---|
|  |  |  |  |  |  |  |  |  |
|  |  |  |  |  |  |  |  |  |
|  |  |  |  |  |  |  |  |  |

**Date:** _____  **Muscle Group:** _____

S  M  T  W  T  F  S    **Start Time** _____
◯  ◯  ◯  ◯  ◯  ◯  ◯

**Weight:** _____   **Finish Time** _____

☐ Upper Body     ☐ Lower Body     ☐ Abs

| Exercise | Set | 1 | 2 | 3 | 4 | 5 | 6 | 7 |
|---|---|---|---|---|---|---|---|---|
|  | Reps |  |  |  |  |  |  |  |
|  | Weight |  |  |  |  |  |  |  |
|  | Reps |  |  |  |  |  |  |  |
|  | Weight |  |  |  |  |  |  |  |
|  | Reps |  |  |  |  |  |  |  |
|  | Weight |  |  |  |  |  |  |  |
|  | Reps |  |  |  |  |  |  |  |
|  | Weight |  |  |  |  |  |  |  |
|  | Reps |  |  |  |  |  |  |  |
|  | Weight |  |  |  |  |  |  |  |
|  | Reps |  |  |  |  |  |  |  |
|  | Weight |  |  |  |  |  |  |  |
|  | Reps |  |  |  |  |  |  |  |
|  | Weight |  |  |  |  |  |  |  |
|  | Reps |  |  |  |  |  |  |  |
|  | Weight |  |  |  |  |  |  |  |

| Cardio | Time | Distance | Heart Rate | Cals Burned |
|---|---|---|---|---|
|  |  |  |  |  |
|  |  |  |  |  |
|  |  |  |  |  |

### Measurements

| Neck | R Bicep | L Bicep | Chest | Waist | Hips | R Thigh | L Thigh | Calf |
|---|---|---|---|---|---|---|---|---|
|  |  |  |  |  |  |  |  |  |
|  |  |  |  |  |  |  |  |  |
|  |  |  |  |  |  |  |  |  |

**Date:** _____   **Muscle Group:** _____

S  M  T  W  T  F  S
○  ○  ○  ○  ○  ○  ○   **Start Time** _____

**Weight:** _____   **Finish Time** _____

☐ Upper Body     ☐ Lower Body     ☐ Abs

| Exercise | Set | 1 | 2 | 3 | 4 | 5 | 6 | 7 |
|---|---|---|---|---|---|---|---|---|
|  | Reps |  |  |  |  |  |  |  |
|  | Weight |  |  |  |  |  |  |  |
|  | Reps |  |  |  |  |  |  |  |
|  | Weight |  |  |  |  |  |  |  |
|  | Reps |  |  |  |  |  |  |  |
|  | Weight |  |  |  |  |  |  |  |
|  | Reps |  |  |  |  |  |  |  |
|  | Weight |  |  |  |  |  |  |  |
|  | Reps |  |  |  |  |  |  |  |
|  | Weight |  |  |  |  |  |  |  |
|  | Reps |  |  |  |  |  |  |  |
|  | Weight |  |  |  |  |  |  |  |
|  | Reps |  |  |  |  |  |  |  |
|  | Weight |  |  |  |  |  |  |  |
|  | Reps |  |  |  |  |  |  |  |
|  | Weight |  |  |  |  |  |  |  |

| Cardio | Time | Distance | Heart Rate | Cals Burned |
|---|---|---|---|---|
|  |  |  |  |  |
|  |  |  |  |  |
|  |  |  |  |  |

### Measurements

| Neck | R Bicep | L Bicep | Chest | Waist | Hips | R Thigh | L Thigh | Calf |
|---|---|---|---|---|---|---|---|---|
|  |  |  |  |  |  |  |  |  |
|  |  |  |  |  |  |  |  |  |
|  |  |  |  |  |  |  |  |  |

**Date:** _____    **Muscle Group:** _____

S  M  T  W  T  F  S    **Start Time** _____
◯  ◯  ◯  ◯  ◯  ◯  ◯

**Weight:** _____    **Finish Time** _____

☐ Upper Body        ☐ Lower Body         ☐ Abs

| Exercise | Set | 1 | 2 | 3 | 4 | 5 | 6 | 7 |
|---|---|---|---|---|---|---|---|---|
|  | Reps |  |  |  |  |  |  |  |
|  | Weight |  |  |  |  |  |  |  |
|  | Reps |  |  |  |  |  |  |  |
|  | Weight |  |  |  |  |  |  |  |
|  | Reps |  |  |  |  |  |  |  |
|  | Weight |  |  |  |  |  |  |  |
|  | Reps |  |  |  |  |  |  |  |
|  | Weight |  |  |  |  |  |  |  |
|  | Reps |  |  |  |  |  |  |  |
|  | Weight |  |  |  |  |  |  |  |
|  | Reps |  |  |  |  |  |  |  |
|  | Weight |  |  |  |  |  |  |  |
|  | Reps |  |  |  |  |  |  |  |
|  | Weight |  |  |  |  |  |  |  |
|  | Reps |  |  |  |  |  |  |  |
|  | Weight |  |  |  |  |  |  |  |

| Cardio | Time | Distance | Heart Rate | Cals Burned |
|---|---|---|---|---|
|  |  |  |  |  |
|  |  |  |  |  |
|  |  |  |  |  |

## Measurements

| Neck | R Bicep | L Bicep | Chest | Waist | Hips | R Thigh | L Thigh | Calf |
|---|---|---|---|---|---|---|---|---|
|  |  |  |  |  |  |  |  |  |
|  |  |  |  |  |  |  |  |  |
|  |  |  |  |  |  |  |  |  |

**Date:** _____  **Muscle Group:** _____

S  M  T  W  T  F  S   **Start Time** _____
○  ○  ○  ○  ○  ○  ○

**Weight:** _____  **Finish Time** _____

☐ Upper Body   ☐ Lower Body   ☐ Abs

| Exercise | Set | 1 | 2 | 3 | 4 | 5 | 6 | 7 |
|---|---|---|---|---|---|---|---|---|
|  | Reps |  |  |  |  |  |  |  |
|  | Weight |  |  |  |  |  |  |  |
|  | Reps |  |  |  |  |  |  |  |
|  | Weight |  |  |  |  |  |  |  |
|  | Reps |  |  |  |  |  |  |  |
|  | Weight |  |  |  |  |  |  |  |
|  | Reps |  |  |  |  |  |  |  |
|  | Weight |  |  |  |  |  |  |  |
|  | Reps |  |  |  |  |  |  |  |
|  | Weight |  |  |  |  |  |  |  |
|  | Reps |  |  |  |  |  |  |  |
|  | Weight |  |  |  |  |  |  |  |
|  | Reps |  |  |  |  |  |  |  |
|  | Weight |  |  |  |  |  |  |  |
|  | Reps |  |  |  |  |  |  |  |
|  | Weight |  |  |  |  |  |  |  |

| Cardio | Time | Distance | Heart Rate | Cals Burned |
|---|---|---|---|---|
|  |  |  |  |  |
|  |  |  |  |  |
|  |  |  |  |  |

## Measurements

| Neck | R Bicep | L Bicep | Chest | Waist | Hips | R Thigh | L Thigh | Calf |
|---|---|---|---|---|---|---|---|---|
|  |  |  |  |  |  |  |  |  |
|  |  |  |  |  |  |  |  |  |
|  |  |  |  |  |  |  |  |  |

Date:_____  Muscle Group: _____

S  M  T  W  T  F  S   Start Time_____
○  ○  ○  ○  ○  ○  ○

Weight:_____   Finish Time_____

☐ Upper Body      ☐ Lower Body      ☐ Abs

| Exercise | Set | 1 | 2 | 3 | 4 | 5 | 6 | 7 |
|---|---|---|---|---|---|---|---|---|
|  | Reps |  |  |  |  |  |  |  |
|  | Weight |  |  |  |  |  |  |  |
|  | Reps |  |  |  |  |  |  |  |
|  | Weight |  |  |  |  |  |  |  |
|  | Reps |  |  |  |  |  |  |  |
|  | Weight |  |  |  |  |  |  |  |
|  | Reps |  |  |  |  |  |  |  |
|  | Weight |  |  |  |  |  |  |  |
|  | Reps |  |  |  |  |  |  |  |
|  | Weight |  |  |  |  |  |  |  |
|  | Reps |  |  |  |  |  |  |  |
|  | Weight |  |  |  |  |  |  |  |
|  | Reps |  |  |  |  |  |  |  |
|  | Weight |  |  |  |  |  |  |  |
|  | Reps |  |  |  |  |  |  |  |
|  | Weight |  |  |  |  |  |  |  |

| Cardio | Time | Distance | Heart Rate | Cals Burned |
|---|---|---|---|---|
|  |  |  |  |  |
|  |  |  |  |  |
|  |  |  |  |  |

## Measurements

| Neck | R Bicep | L Bicep | Chest | Waist | Hips | R Thigh | L Thigh | Calf |
|---|---|---|---|---|---|---|---|---|
|  |  |  |  |  |  |  |  |  |
|  |  |  |  |  |  |  |  |  |
|  |  |  |  |  |  |  |  |  |

Date: _____  Muscle Group: _____

S M T W T F S  Start Time _____
○ ○ ○ ○ ○ ○ ○

Weight: _____  Finish Time _____

☐ Upper Body   ☐ Lower Body   ☐ Abs

| Exercise | Set | 1 | 2 | 3 | 4 | 5 | 6 | 7 |
|---|---|---|---|---|---|---|---|---|
|  | Reps |  |  |  |  |  |  |  |
|  | Weight |  |  |  |  |  |  |  |
|  | Reps |  |  |  |  |  |  |  |
|  | Weight |  |  |  |  |  |  |  |
|  | Reps |  |  |  |  |  |  |  |
|  | Weight |  |  |  |  |  |  |  |
|  | Reps |  |  |  |  |  |  |  |
|  | Weight |  |  |  |  |  |  |  |
|  | Reps |  |  |  |  |  |  |  |
|  | Weight |  |  |  |  |  |  |  |
|  | Reps |  |  |  |  |  |  |  |
|  | Weight |  |  |  |  |  |  |  |
|  | Reps |  |  |  |  |  |  |  |
|  | Weight |  |  |  |  |  |  |  |
|  | Reps |  |  |  |  |  |  |  |
|  | Weight |  |  |  |  |  |  |  |

| Cardio | Time | Distance | Heart Rate | Cals Burned |
|---|---|---|---|---|
|  |  |  |  |  |
|  |  |  |  |  |
|  |  |  |  |  |

## Measurements

| Neck | R Bicep | L Bicep | Chest | Waist | Hips | R Thigh | L Thigh | Calf |
|---|---|---|---|---|---|---|---|---|
|  |  |  |  |  |  |  |  |  |
|  |  |  |  |  |  |  |  |  |
|  |  |  |  |  |  |  |  |  |

**Date:** _____  **Muscle Group:** _____

S   M   T   W   T   F   S    **Start Time** _____
○   ○   ○   ○   ○   ○   ○

**Weight:** _____   **Finish Time** _____

☐ **Upper Body**   ☐ **Lower Body**   ☐ **Abs**

| Exercise | Set | 1 | 2 | 3 | 4 | 5 | 6 | 7 |
|---|---|---|---|---|---|---|---|---|
|  | Reps |  |  |  |  |  |  |  |
|  | Weight |  |  |  |  |  |  |  |
|  | Reps |  |  |  |  |  |  |  |
|  | Weight |  |  |  |  |  |  |  |
|  | Reps |  |  |  |  |  |  |  |
|  | Weight |  |  |  |  |  |  |  |
|  | Reps |  |  |  |  |  |  |  |
|  | Weight |  |  |  |  |  |  |  |
|  | Reps |  |  |  |  |  |  |  |
|  | Weight |  |  |  |  |  |  |  |
|  | Reps |  |  |  |  |  |  |  |
|  | Weight |  |  |  |  |  |  |  |
|  | Reps |  |  |  |  |  |  |  |
|  | Weight |  |  |  |  |  |  |  |
|  | Reps |  |  |  |  |  |  |  |
|  | Weight |  |  |  |  |  |  |  |

| Cardio | Time | Distance | Heart Rate | Cals Burned |
|---|---|---|---|---|
|  |  |  |  |  |
|  |  |  |  |  |
|  |  |  |  |  |

## Measurements

| Neck | R Bicep | L Bicep | Chest | Waist | Hips | R Thigh | L Thigh | Calf |
|---|---|---|---|---|---|---|---|---|
|  |  |  |  |  |  |  |  |  |
|  |  |  |  |  |  |  |  |  |
|  |  |  |  |  |  |  |  |  |

Date:_____ Muscle Group: _____

S  M  T  W  T  F  S   Start Time_____
○  ○  ○  ○  ○  ○  ○

Weight:_____ Finish Time_____

☐ Upper Body    ☐ Lower Body    ☐ Abs

| Exercise | Set | 1 | 2 | 3 | 4 | 5 | 6 | 7 |
|---|---|---|---|---|---|---|---|---|
| | Reps | | | | | | | |
| | Weight | | | | | | | |
| | Reps | | | | | | | |
| | Weight | | | | | | | |
| | Reps | | | | | | | |
| | Weight | | | | | | | |
| | Reps | | | | | | | |
| | Weight | | | | | | | |
| | Reps | | | | | | | |
| | Weight | | | | | | | |
| | Reps | | | | | | | |
| | Weight | | | | | | | |
| | Reps | | | | | | | |
| | Weight | | | | | | | |
| | Reps | | | | | | | |
| | Weight | | | | | | | |

| Cardio | Time | Distance | Heart Rate | Cals Burned |
|---|---|---|---|---|
| | | | | |
| | | | | |
| | | | | |

## Measurements

| Neck | R Bicep | L Bicep | Chest | Waist | Hips | R Thigh | L Thigh | Calf |
|---|---|---|---|---|---|---|---|---|
| | | | | | | | | |
| | | | | | | | | |
| | | | | | | | | |

Date: _____    Muscle Group: _____

S  M  T  W  T  F  S     Start Time _____
○  ○  ○  ○  ○  ○  ○

Weight: _____    Finish Time _____

☐ Upper Body     ☐ Lower Body     ☐ Abs

| Exercise | Set | 1 | 2 | 3 | 4 | 5 | 6 | 7 |
|---|---|---|---|---|---|---|---|---|
|  | Reps |  |  |  |  |  |  |  |
|  | Weight |  |  |  |  |  |  |  |
|  | Reps |  |  |  |  |  |  |  |
|  | Weight |  |  |  |  |  |  |  |
|  | Reps |  |  |  |  |  |  |  |
|  | Weight |  |  |  |  |  |  |  |
|  | Reps |  |  |  |  |  |  |  |
|  | Weight |  |  |  |  |  |  |  |
|  | Reps |  |  |  |  |  |  |  |
|  | Weight |  |  |  |  |  |  |  |
|  | Rcps |  |  |  |  |  |  |  |
|  | Weight |  |  |  |  |  |  |  |
|  | Reps |  |  |  |  |  |  |  |
|  | Weight |  |  |  |  |  |  |  |
|  | Reps |  |  |  |  |  |  |  |
|  | Weight |  |  |  |  |  |  |  |

| Cardio | Time | Distance | Heart Rate | Cals Burned |
|---|---|---|---|---|
|  |  |  |  |  |
|  |  |  |  |  |
|  |  |  |  |  |

### Measurements

| Neck | R Bicep | L Bicep | Chest | Waist | Hips | R Thigh | L Thigh | Calf |
|---|---|---|---|---|---|---|---|---|
|  |  |  |  |  |  |  |  |  |
|  |  |  |  |  |  |  |  |  |
|  |  |  |  |  |  |  |  |  |

**Date:** _____   **Muscle Group:** _____

S  M  T  W  T  F  S   **Start Time** _____
◯  ◯  ◯  ◯  ◯  ◯  ◯

**Weight:** _____   **Finish Time** _____

☐ Upper Body   ☐ Lower Body   ☐ Abs

| Exercise | Set | 1 | 2 | 3 | 4 | 5 | 6 | 7 |
|---|---|---|---|---|---|---|---|---|
|  | Reps |  |  |  |  |  |  |  |
|  | Weight |  |  |  |  |  |  |  |
|  | Reps |  |  |  |  |  |  |  |
|  | Weight |  |  |  |  |  |  |  |
|  | Reps |  |  |  |  |  |  |  |
|  | Weight |  |  |  |  |  |  |  |
|  | Reps |  |  |  |  |  |  |  |
|  | Weight |  |  |  |  |  |  |  |
|  | Reps |  |  |  |  |  |  |  |
|  | Weight |  |  |  |  |  |  |  |
|  | Reps |  |  |  |  |  |  |  |
|  | Weight |  |  |  |  |  |  |  |
|  | Reps |  |  |  |  |  |  |  |
|  | Weight |  |  |  |  |  |  |  |
|  | Reps |  |  |  |  |  |  |  |
|  | Weight |  |  |  |  |  |  |  |

| Cardio | Time | Distance | Heart Rate | Cals Burned |
|---|---|---|---|---|
|  |  |  |  |  |
|  |  |  |  |  |
|  |  |  |  |  |

### Measurements

| Neck | R Bicep | L Bicep | Chest | Waist | Hips | R Thigh | L Thigh | Calf |
|---|---|---|---|---|---|---|---|---|
|  |  |  |  |  |  |  |  |  |
|  |  |  |  |  |  |  |  |  |
|  |  |  |  |  |  |  |  |  |

**Date:** _____  **Muscle Group:** _____

S M T W T F S  **Start Time** _____
○ ○ ○ ○ ○ ○ ○

**Weight:** _____  **Finish Time** _____

☐ **Upper Body**    ☐ **Lower Body**    ☐ **Abs**

| Exercise | Set | 1 | 2 | 3 | 4 | 5 | 6 | 7 |
|---|---|---|---|---|---|---|---|---|
|  | Reps |  |  |  |  |  |  |  |
|  | Weight |  |  |  |  |  |  |  |
|  | Reps |  |  |  |  |  |  |  |
|  | Weight |  |  |  |  |  |  |  |
|  | Reps |  |  |  |  |  |  |  |
|  | Weight |  |  |  |  |  |  |  |
|  | Reps |  |  |  |  |  |  |  |
|  | Weight |  |  |  |  |  |  |  |
|  | Reps |  |  |  |  |  |  |  |
|  | Weight |  |  |  |  |  |  |  |
|  | Reps |  |  |  |  |  |  |  |
|  | Weight |  |  |  |  |  |  |  |
|  | Reps |  |  |  |  |  |  |  |
|  | Weight |  |  |  |  |  |  |  |
|  | Reps |  |  |  |  |  |  |  |
|  | Weight |  |  |  |  |  |  |  |

| Cardio | Time | Distance | Heart Rate | Cals Burned |
|---|---|---|---|---|
|  |  |  |  |  |
|  |  |  |  |  |
|  |  |  |  |  |

### Measurements

| Neck | R Bicep | L Bicep | Chest | Waist | Hips | R Thigh | L Thigh | Calf |
|---|---|---|---|---|---|---|---|---|
|  |  |  |  |  |  |  |  |  |
|  |  |  |  |  |  |  |  |  |
|  |  |  |  |  |  |  |  |  |

**Date:** _____  **Muscle Group:** _____

S M T W T F S  **Start Time** _____
○ ○ ○ ○ ○ ○ ○

**Weight:** _____  **Finish Time** _____

☐ Upper Body   ☐ Lower Body   ☐ Abs

| Exercise | Set | 1 | 2 | 3 | 4 | 5 | 6 | 7 |
|---|---|---|---|---|---|---|---|---|
| | Reps | | | | | | | |
| | Weight | | | | | | | |
| | Reps | | | | | | | |
| | Weight | | | | | | | |
| | Reps | | | | | | | |
| | Weight | | | | | | | |
| | Reps | | | | | | | |
| | Weight | | | | | | | |
| | Reps | | | | | | | |
| | Weight | | | | | | | |
| | Reps | | | | | | | |
| | Weight | | | | | | | |
| | Reps | | | | | | | |
| | Weight | | | | | | | |
| | Reps | | | | | | | |
| | Weight | | | | | | | |

| Cardio | Time | Distance | Heart Rate | Cals Burned |
|---|---|---|---|---|
| | | | | |
| | | | | |
| | | | | |

## Measurements

| Neck | R Bicep | L Bicep | Chest | Waist | Hips | R Thigh | L Thigh | Calf |
|---|---|---|---|---|---|---|---|---|
| | | | | | | | | |
| | | | | | | | | |
| | | | | | | | | |

**Date:**_____  **Muscle Group:** _____

S   M   T   W   T   F   S   **Start Time** _____
○   ○   ○   ○   ○   ○   ○

**Weight:** _____  **Finish Time** _____

☐ **Upper Body**    ☐ **Lower Body**    ☐ **Abs**

| Exercise | Set | 1 | 2 | 3 | 4 | 5 | 6 | 7 |
|---|---|---|---|---|---|---|---|---|
|  | Reps |  |  |  |  |  |  |  |
|  | Weight |  |  |  |  |  |  |  |
|  | Reps |  |  |  |  |  |  |  |
|  | Weight |  |  |  |  |  |  |  |
|  | Reps |  |  |  |  |  |  |  |
|  | Weight |  |  |  |  |  |  |  |
|  | Reps |  |  |  |  |  |  |  |
|  | Weight |  |  |  |  |  |  |  |
|  | Reps |  |  |  |  |  |  |  |
|  | Weight |  |  |  |  |  |  |  |
|  | Reps |  |  |  |  |  |  |  |
|  | Weight |  |  |  |  |  |  |  |
|  | Reps |  |  |  |  |  |  |  |
|  | Weight |  |  |  |  |  |  |  |
|  | Reps |  |  |  |  |  |  |  |
|  | Weight |  |  |  |  |  |  |  |

| Cardio | Time | Distance | Heart Rate | Cals Burned |
|---|---|---|---|---|
|  |  |  |  |  |
|  |  |  |  |  |
|  |  |  |  |  |

## Measurements

| Neck | R Bicep | L Bicep | Chest | Waist | Hips | R Thigh | L Thigh | Calf |
|---|---|---|---|---|---|---|---|---|
|  |  |  |  |  |  |  |  |  |
|  |  |  |  |  |  |  |  |  |
|  |  |  |  |  |  |  |  |  |

**Date:** _____  **Muscle Group:** _____

S  M  T  W  T  F  S    **Start Time** _____
◯ ◯ ◯ ◯ ◯ ◯ ◯

**Weight:** _____  **Finish Time** _____

☐ **Upper Body**   ☐ **Lower Body**   ☐ **Abs**

| Exercise | Set | 1 | 2 | 3 | 4 | 5 | 6 | 7 |
|---|---|---|---|---|---|---|---|---|
|  | Reps |  |  |  |  |  |  |  |
|  | Weight |  |  |  |  |  |  |  |
|  | Reps |  |  |  |  |  |  |  |
|  | Weight |  |  |  |  |  |  |  |
|  | Reps |  |  |  |  |  |  |  |
|  | Weight |  |  |  |  |  |  |  |
|  | Reps |  |  |  |  |  |  |  |
|  | Weight |  |  |  |  |  |  |  |
|  | Reps |  |  |  |  |  |  |  |
|  | Weight |  |  |  |  |  |  |  |
|  | Reps |  |  |  |  |  |  |  |
|  | Weight |  |  |  |  |  |  |  |
|  | Reps |  |  |  |  |  |  |  |
|  | Weight |  |  |  |  |  |  |  |
|  | Reps |  |  |  |  |  |  |  |
|  | Weight |  |  |  |  |  |  |  |

| Cardio | Time | Distance | Heart Rate | Cals Burned |
|---|---|---|---|---|
|  |  |  |  |  |
|  |  |  |  |  |
|  |  |  |  |  |

## Measurements

| Neck | R Bicep | L Bicep | Chest | Waist | Hips | R Thigh | L Thigh | Calf |
|---|---|---|---|---|---|---|---|---|
|  |  |  |  |  |  |  |  |  |
|  |  |  |  |  |  |  |  |  |
|  |  |  |  |  |  |  |  |  |

**Date:** _____  **Muscle Group:** _____

S M T W T F S   **Start Time** _____
○ ○ ○ ○ ○ ○ ○

**Weight:** _____  **Finish Time** _____

☐ Upper Body   ☐ Lower Body   ☐ Abs

| Exercise | Set | 1 | 2 | 3 | 4 | 5 | 6 | 7 |
|---|---|---|---|---|---|---|---|---|
|  | Reps |  |  |  |  |  |  |  |
|  | Weight |  |  |  |  |  |  |  |
|  | Reps |  |  |  |  |  |  |  |
|  | Weight |  |  |  |  |  |  |  |
|  | Reps |  |  |  |  |  |  |  |
|  | Weight |  |  |  |  |  |  |  |
|  | Reps |  |  |  |  |  |  |  |
|  | Weight |  |  |  |  |  |  |  |
|  | Reps |  |  |  |  |  |  |  |
|  | Weight |  |  |  |  |  |  |  |
|  | Rcps |  |  |  |  |  |  |  |
|  | Weight |  |  |  |  |  |  |  |
|  | Reps |  |  |  |  |  |  |  |
|  | Weight |  |  |  |  |  |  |  |
|  | Reps |  |  |  |  |  |  |  |
|  | Weight |  |  |  |  |  |  |  |

| Cardio | Time | Distance | Heart Rate | Cals Burned |
|---|---|---|---|---|
|  |  |  |  |  |
|  |  |  |  |  |
|  |  |  |  |  |

### Measurements

| Neck | R Bicep | L Bicep | Chest | Waist | Hips | R Thigh | L Thigh | Calf |
|---|---|---|---|---|---|---|---|---|
|  |  |  |  |  |  |  |  |  |
|  |  |  |  |  |  |  |  |  |
|  |  |  |  |  |  |  |  |  |

**Date:** _____  **Muscle Group:** _____

S  M  T  W  T  F  S  **Start Time** _____
○  ○  ○  ○  ○  ○  ○

**Weight:** _____  **Finish Time** _____

☐ Upper Body   ☐ Lower Body   ☐ Abs

| Exercise | Set | 1 | 2 | 3 | 4 | 5 | 6 | 7 |
|---|---|---|---|---|---|---|---|---|
|  | Reps |  |  |  |  |  |  |  |
|  | Weight |  |  |  |  |  |  |  |
|  | Reps |  |  |  |  |  |  |  |
|  | Weight |  |  |  |  |  |  |  |
|  | Reps |  |  |  |  |  |  |  |
|  | Weight |  |  |  |  |  |  |  |
|  | Reps |  |  |  |  |  |  |  |
|  | Weight |  |  |  |  |  |  |  |
|  | Reps |  |  |  |  |  |  |  |
|  | Weight |  |  |  |  |  |  |  |
|  | Reps |  |  |  |  |  |  |  |
|  | Weight |  |  |  |  |  |  |  |
|  | Reps |  |  |  |  |  |  |  |
|  | Weight |  |  |  |  |  |  |  |
|  | Reps |  |  |  |  |  |  |  |
|  | Weight |  |  |  |  |  |  |  |

| Cardio | Time | Distance | Heart Rate | Cals Burned |
|---|---|---|---|---|
|  |  |  |  |  |
|  |  |  |  |  |
|  |  |  |  |  |

### Measurements

| Neck | R Bicep | L Bicep | Chest | Waist | Hips | R Thigh | L Thigh | Calf |
|---|---|---|---|---|---|---|---|---|
|  |  |  |  |  |  |  |  |  |
|  |  |  |  |  |  |  |  |  |
|  |  |  |  |  |  |  |  |  |

Date: _____  Muscle Group: _____

S  M  T  W  T  F  S
○  ○  ○  ○  ○  ○  ○

Weight: _____  Start Time _____

Finish Time _____

☐ Upper Body   ☐ Lower Body   ☐ Abs

| Exercise | Set | 1 | 2 | 3 | 4 | 5 | 6 | 7 |
|---|---|---|---|---|---|---|---|---|
|  | Reps |  |  |  |  |  |  |  |
|  | Weight |  |  |  |  |  |  |  |
|  | Reps |  |  |  |  |  |  |  |
|  | Weight |  |  |  |  |  |  |  |
|  | Reps |  |  |  |  |  |  |  |
|  | Weight |  |  |  |  |  |  |  |
|  | Reps |  |  |  |  |  |  |  |
|  | Weight |  |  |  |  |  |  |  |
|  | Reps |  |  |  |  |  |  |  |
|  | Weight |  |  |  |  |  |  |  |
|  | Reps |  |  |  |  |  |  |  |
|  | Weight |  |  |  |  |  |  |  |
|  | Reps |  |  |  |  |  |  |  |
|  | Weight |  |  |  |  |  |  |  |
|  | Reps |  |  |  |  |  |  |  |
|  | Weight |  |  |  |  |  |  |  |

| Cardio | Time | Distance | Heart Rate | Cals Burned |
|---|---|---|---|---|
|  |  |  |  |  |
|  |  |  |  |  |
|  |  |  |  |  |

## Measurements

| Neck | R Bicep | L Bicep | Chest | Waist | Hips | R Thigh | L Thigh | Calf |
|---|---|---|---|---|---|---|---|---|
|  |  |  |  |  |  |  |  |  |
|  |  |  |  |  |  |  |  |  |
|  |  |  |  |  |  |  |  |  |

**Date:** _____   **Muscle Group:** _____

S  M  T  W  T  F  S   **Start Time** _____
○  ○  ○  ○  ○  ○  ○

**Weight:** _____   **Finish Time** _____

☐ **Upper Body**    ☐ **Lower Body**    ☐ **Abs**

| Exercise | Set | 1 | 2 | 3 | 4 | 5 | 6 | 7 |
|---|---|---|---|---|---|---|---|---|
|  | Reps |  |  |  |  |  |  |  |
|  | Weight |  |  |  |  |  |  |  |
|  | Reps |  |  |  |  |  |  |  |
|  | Weight |  |  |  |  |  |  |  |
|  | Reps |  |  |  |  |  |  |  |
|  | Weight |  |  |  |  |  |  |  |
|  | Reps |  |  |  |  |  |  |  |
|  | Weight |  |  |  |  |  |  |  |
|  | Reps |  |  |  |  |  |  |  |
|  | Weight |  |  |  |  |  |  |  |
|  | Reps |  |  |  |  |  |  |  |
|  | Weight |  |  |  |  |  |  |  |
|  | Reps |  |  |  |  |  |  |  |
|  | Weight |  |  |  |  |  |  |  |
|  | Reps |  |  |  |  |  |  |  |
|  | Weight |  |  |  |  |  |  |  |

| Cardio | Time | Distance | Heart Rate | Cals Burned |
|---|---|---|---|---|
|  |  |  |  |  |
|  |  |  |  |  |
|  |  |  |  |  |

## Measurements

| Neck | R Bicep | L Bicep | Chest | Waist | Hips | R Thigh | L Thigh | Calf |
|---|---|---|---|---|---|---|---|---|
|  |  |  |  |  |  |  |  |  |
|  |  |  |  |  |  |  |  |  |
|  |  |  |  |  |  |  |  |  |

**Date:** _____  **Muscle Group:** _____

S  M  T  W  T  F  S
◯  ◯  ◯  ◯  ◯  ◯  ◯

**Start Time** _____

**Weight:** _____  **Finish Time** _____

☐ Upper Body   ☐ Lower Body   ☐ Abs

| Exercise | Set | 1 | 2 | 3 | 4 | 5 | 6 | 7 |
|---|---|---|---|---|---|---|---|---|
|  | Reps |  |  |  |  |  |  |  |
|  | Weight |  |  |  |  |  |  |  |
|  | Reps |  |  |  |  |  |  |  |
|  | Weight |  |  |  |  |  |  |  |
|  | Reps |  |  |  |  |  |  |  |
|  | Weight |  |  |  |  |  |  |  |
|  | Reps |  |  |  |  |  |  |  |
|  | Weight |  |  |  |  |  |  |  |
|  | Reps |  |  |  |  |  |  |  |
|  | Weight |  |  |  |  |  |  |  |
|  | Rops |  |  |  |  |  |  |  |
|  | Weight |  |  |  |  |  |  |  |
|  | Reps |  |  |  |  |  |  |  |
|  | Weight |  |  |  |  |  |  |  |
|  | Reps |  |  |  |  |  |  |  |
|  | Weight |  |  |  |  |  |  |  |

| Cardio | Time | Distance | Heart Rate | Cals Burned |
|---|---|---|---|---|
|  |  |  |  |  |
|  |  |  |  |  |
|  |  |  |  |  |

### Measurements

| Neck | R Bicep | L Bicep | Chest | Waist | Hips | R Thigh | L Thigh | Calf |
|---|---|---|---|---|---|---|---|---|
|  |  |  |  |  |  |  |  |  |
|  |  |  |  |  |  |  |  |  |
|  |  |  |  |  |  |  |  |  |

**Date:** _____  **Muscle Group:** _____

S  M  T  W  T  F  S  **Start Time** _____
○  ○  ○  ○  ○  ○  ○

**Weight:** _____  **Finish Time** _____

☐ Upper Body  ☐ Lower Body  ☐ Abs

| Exercise | Set | 1 | 2 | 3 | 4 | 5 | 6 | 7 |
|---|---|---|---|---|---|---|---|---|
|  | Reps |  |  |  |  |  |  |  |
|  | Weight |  |  |  |  |  |  |  |
|  | Reps |  |  |  |  |  |  |  |
|  | Weight |  |  |  |  |  |  |  |
|  | Reps |  |  |  |  |  |  |  |
|  | Weight |  |  |  |  |  |  |  |
|  | Reps |  |  |  |  |  |  |  |
|  | Weight |  |  |  |  |  |  |  |
|  | Reps |  |  |  |  |  |  |  |
|  | Weight |  |  |  |  |  |  |  |
|  | Reps |  |  |  |  |  |  |  |
|  | Weight |  |  |  |  |  |  |  |
|  | Reps |  |  |  |  |  |  |  |
|  | Weight |  |  |  |  |  |  |  |
|  | Reps |  |  |  |  |  |  |  |
|  | Weight |  |  |  |  |  |  |  |

| Cardio | Time | Distance | Heart Rate | Cals Burned |
|---|---|---|---|---|
|  |  |  |  |  |
|  |  |  |  |  |
|  |  |  |  |  |

### Measurements

| Neck | R Bicep | L Bicep | Chest | Waist | Hips | R Thigh | L Thigh | Calf |
|---|---|---|---|---|---|---|---|---|
|  |  |  |  |  |  |  |  |  |
|  |  |  |  |  |  |  |  |  |
|  |  |  |  |  |  |  |  |  |

Date:_____ Muscle Group: _____

S M T W T F S  Start Time_____
○ ○ ○ ○ ○ ○ ○

Weight:_____ Finish Time_____

☐ Upper Body    ☐ Lower Body    ☐ Abs

| Exercise | Set | 1 | 2 | 3 | 4 | 5 | 6 | 7 |
|---|---|---|---|---|---|---|---|---|
|  | Reps |  |  |  |  |  |  |  |
|  | Weight |  |  |  |  |  |  |  |
|  | Reps |  |  |  |  |  |  |  |
|  | Weight |  |  |  |  |  |  |  |
|  | Reps |  |  |  |  |  |  |  |
|  | Weight |  |  |  |  |  |  |  |
|  | Reps |  |  |  |  |  |  |  |
|  | Weight |  |  |  |  |  |  |  |
|  | Reps |  |  |  |  |  |  |  |
|  | Weight |  |  |  |  |  |  |  |
|  | Reps |  |  |  |  |  |  |  |
|  | Weight |  |  |  |  |  |  |  |
|  | Reps |  |  |  |  |  |  |  |
|  | Weight |  |  |  |  |  |  |  |
|  | Reps |  |  |  |  |  |  |  |
|  | Weight |  |  |  |  |  |  |  |

| Cardio | Time | Distance | Heart Rate | Cals Burned |
|---|---|---|---|---|
|  |  |  |  |  |
|  |  |  |  |  |
|  |  |  |  |  |

### Measurements

| Neck | R Bicep | L Bicep | Chest | Waist | Hips | R Thigh | L Thigh | Calf |
|---|---|---|---|---|---|---|---|---|
|  |  |  |  |  |  |  |  |  |
|  |  |  |  |  |  |  |  |  |
|  |  |  |  |  |  |  |  |  |

**Date:** _____  **Muscle Group:** _____

S M T W T F S  **Start Time** _____
○ ○ ○ ○ ○ ○ ○

**Weight:** _____  **Finish Time** _____

☐ Upper Body   ☐ Lower Body   ☐ Abs

| Exercise | Set | 1 | 2 | 3 | 4 | 5 | 6 | 7 |
|---|---|---|---|---|---|---|---|---|
|  | Reps |  |  |  |  |  |  |  |
|  | Weight |  |  |  |  |  |  |  |
|  | Reps |  |  |  |  |  |  |  |
|  | Weight |  |  |  |  |  |  |  |
|  | Reps |  |  |  |  |  |  |  |
|  | Weight |  |  |  |  |  |  |  |
|  | Reps |  |  |  |  |  |  |  |
|  | Weight |  |  |  |  |  |  |  |
|  | Reps |  |  |  |  |  |  |  |
|  | Weight |  |  |  |  |  |  |  |
|  | Reps |  |  |  |  |  |  |  |
|  | Weight |  |  |  |  |  |  |  |
|  | Reps |  |  |  |  |  |  |  |
|  | Weight |  |  |  |  |  |  |  |
|  | Reps |  |  |  |  |  |  |  |
|  | Weight |  |  |  |  |  |  |  |

| Cardio | Time | Distance | Heart Rate | Cals Burned |
|---|---|---|---|---|
|  |  |  |  |  |
|  |  |  |  |  |
|  |  |  |  |  |

### Measurements

| Neck | R Bicep | L Bicep | Chest | Waist | Hips | R Thigh | L Thigh | Calf |
|---|---|---|---|---|---|---|---|---|
|  |  |  |  |  |  |  |  |  |
|  |  |  |  |  |  |  |  |  |
|  |  |  |  |  |  |  |  |  |

Date:_____ Muscle Group:_____

S M T W T F S   Start Time_____
○ ○ ○ ○ ○ ○ ○

Weight:_____ Finish Time_____

☐ Upper Body    ☐ Lower Body    ☐ Abs

| Exercise | Set | 1 | 2 | 3 | 4 | 5 | 6 | 7 |
|---|---|---|---|---|---|---|---|---|
| | Reps | | | | | | | |
| | Weight | | | | | | | |
| | Reps | | | | | | | |
| | Weight | | | | | | | |
| | Reps | | | | | | | |
| | Weight | | | | | | | |
| | Reps | | | | | | | |
| | Weight | | | | | | | |
| | Reps | | | | | | | |
| | Weight | | | | | | | |
| | Reps | | | | | | | |
| | Weight | | | | | | | |
| | Reps | | | | | | | |
| | Weight | | | | | | | |
| | Reps | | | | | | | |
| | Weight | | | | | | | |

| Cardio | Time | Distance | Heart Rate | Cals Burned |
|---|---|---|---|---|
| | | | | |
| | | | | |
| | | | | |

## Measurements

| Neck | R Bicep | L Bicep | Chest | Waist | Hips | R Thigh | L Thigh | Calf |
|---|---|---|---|---|---|---|---|---|
| | | | | | | | | |
| | | | | | | | | |
| | | | | | | | | |

**Date:** _____  **Muscle Group:** _____

S  M  T  W  T  F  S
○  ○  ○  ○  ○  ○  ○

**Start Time** _____

**Weight:** _____

**Finish Time** _____

☐ Upper Body  ☐ Lower Body  ☐ Abs

| Exercise | Set | 1 | 2 | 3 | 4 | 5 | 6 | 7 |
|---|---|---|---|---|---|---|---|---|
|  | Reps |  |  |  |  |  |  |  |
|  | Weight |  |  |  |  |  |  |  |
|  | Reps |  |  |  |  |  |  |  |
|  | Weight |  |  |  |  |  |  |  |
|  | Reps |  |  |  |  |  |  |  |
|  | Weight |  |  |  |  |  |  |  |
|  | Reps |  |  |  |  |  |  |  |
|  | Weight |  |  |  |  |  |  |  |
|  | Reps |  |  |  |  |  |  |  |
|  | Weight |  |  |  |  |  |  |  |
|  | Reps |  |  |  |  |  |  |  |
|  | Weight |  |  |  |  |  |  |  |
|  | Reps |  |  |  |  |  |  |  |
|  | Weight |  |  |  |  |  |  |  |
|  | Reps |  |  |  |  |  |  |  |
|  | Weight |  |  |  |  |  |  |  |

| Cardio | Time | Distance | Heart Rate | Cals Burned |
|---|---|---|---|---|
|  |  |  |  |  |
|  |  |  |  |  |
|  |  |  |  |  |

## Measurements

| Neck | R Bicep | L Bicep | Chest | Waist | Hips | R Thigh | L Thigh | Calf |
|---|---|---|---|---|---|---|---|---|
|  |  |  |  |  |  |  |  |  |
|  |  |  |  |  |  |  |  |  |
|  |  |  |  |  |  |  |  |  |

# Date:_____  Muscle Group:_____

S M T W T F S  Start Time_____
○ ○ ○ ○ ○ ○ ○

Weight:_____  Finish Time_____

☐ Upper Body  ☐ Lower Body  ☐ Abs

| Exercise | Set | 1 | 2 | 3 | 4 | 5 | 6 | 7 |
|---|---|---|---|---|---|---|---|---|
|  | Reps |  |  |  |  |  |  |  |
|  | Weight |  |  |  |  |  |  |  |
|  | Reps |  |  |  |  |  |  |  |
|  | Weight |  |  |  |  |  |  |  |
|  | Reps |  |  |  |  |  |  |  |
|  | Weight |  |  |  |  |  |  |  |
|  | Reps |  |  |  |  |  |  |  |
|  | Weight |  |  |  |  |  |  |  |
|  | Reps |  |  |  |  |  |  |  |
|  | Weight |  |  |  |  |  |  |  |
|  | Reps |  |  |  |  |  |  |  |
|  | Weight |  |  |  |  |  |  |  |
|  | Reps |  |  |  |  |  |  |  |
|  | Weight |  |  |  |  |  |  |  |
|  | Reps |  |  |  |  |  |  |  |
|  | Weight |  |  |  |  |  |  |  |

| Cardio | Time | Distance | Heart Rate | Cals Burned |
|---|---|---|---|---|
|  |  |  |  |  |
|  |  |  |  |  |
|  |  |  |  |  |

## Measurements

| Neck | R Bicep | L Bicep | Chest | Waist | Hips | R Thigh | L Thigh | Calf |
|---|---|---|---|---|---|---|---|---|
|  |  |  |  |  |  |  |  |  |
|  |  |  |  |  |  |  |  |  |
|  |  |  |  |  |  |  |  |  |

**Date:** _____  **Muscle Group:** _____

S  M  T  W  T  F  S  **Start Time** _____
○  ○  ○  ○  ○  ○  ○

**Weight:** _____  **Finish Time** _____

☐ Upper Body    ☐ Lower Body    ☐ Abs

| Exercise | Set | 1 | 2 | 3 | 4 | 5 | 6 | 7 |
|---|---|---|---|---|---|---|---|---|
|  | Reps |  |  |  |  |  |  |  |
|  | Weight |  |  |  |  |  |  |  |
|  | Reps |  |  |  |  |  |  |  |
|  | Weight |  |  |  |  |  |  |  |
|  | Reps |  |  |  |  |  |  |  |
|  | Weight |  |  |  |  |  |  |  |
|  | Reps |  |  |  |  |  |  |  |
|  | Weight |  |  |  |  |  |  |  |
|  | Reps |  |  |  |  |  |  |  |
|  | Weight |  |  |  |  |  |  |  |
|  | Reps |  |  |  |  |  |  |  |
|  | Weight |  |  |  |  |  |  |  |
|  | Reps |  |  |  |  |  |  |  |
|  | Weight |  |  |  |  |  |  |  |
|  | Reps |  |  |  |  |  |  |  |
|  | Weight |  |  |  |  |  |  |  |

| Cardio | Time | Distance | Heart Rate | Cals Burned |
|---|---|---|---|---|
|  |  |  |  |  |
|  |  |  |  |  |
|  |  |  |  |  |

### Measurements

| Neck | R Bicep | L Bicep | Chest | Waist | Hips | R Thigh | L Thigh | Calf |
|---|---|---|---|---|---|---|---|---|
|  |  |  |  |  |  |  |  |  |
|  |  |  |  |  |  |  |  |  |
|  |  |  |  |  |  |  |  |  |

Date: _____ Muscle Group: _____

S M T W T F S  Start Time _____
○ ○ ○ ○ ○ ○ ○

Weight: _____ Finish Time _____

☐ Upper Body   ☐ Lower Body   ☐ Abs

| Exercise | Set | 1 | 2 | 3 | 4 | 5 | 6 | 7 |
|---|---|---|---|---|---|---|---|---|
|  | Reps |  |  |  |  |  |  |  |
|  | Weight |  |  |  |  |  |  |  |
|  | Reps |  |  |  |  |  |  |  |
|  | Weight |  |  |  |  |  |  |  |
|  | Reps |  |  |  |  |  |  |  |
|  | Weight |  |  |  |  |  |  |  |
|  | Reps |  |  |  |  |  |  |  |
|  | Weight |  |  |  |  |  |  |  |
|  | Reps |  |  |  |  |  |  |  |
|  | Weight |  |  |  |  |  |  |  |
|  | Reps |  |  |  |  |  |  |  |
|  | Weight |  |  |  |  |  |  |  |
|  | Reps |  |  |  |  |  |  |  |
|  | Weight |  |  |  |  |  |  |  |
|  | Reps |  |  |  |  |  |  |  |
|  | Weight |  |  |  |  |  |  |  |

| Cardio | Time | Distance | Heart Rate | Cals Burned |
|---|---|---|---|---|
|  |  |  |  |  |
|  |  |  |  |  |
|  |  |  |  |  |

## Measurements

| Neck | R Bicep | L Bicep | Chest | Waist | Hips | R Thigh | L Thigh | Calf |
|---|---|---|---|---|---|---|---|---|
|  |  |  |  |  |  |  |  |  |
|  |  |  |  |  |  |  |  |  |
|  |  |  |  |  |  |  |  |  |

Date:_____  Muscle Group: _____

S  M  T  W  T  F  S   Start Time_____
○  ○  ○  ○  ○  ○  ○

Weight:_____  Finish Time_____

☐ Upper Body     ☐ Lower Body          ☐ Abs

| Exercise | Set | 1 | 2 | 3 | 4 | 5 | 6 | 7 |
|---|---|---|---|---|---|---|---|---|
|  | Reps |  |  |  |  |  |  |  |
|  | Weight |  |  |  |  |  |  |  |
|  | Reps |  |  |  |  |  |  |  |
|  | Weight |  |  |  |  |  |  |  |
|  | Reps |  |  |  |  |  |  |  |
|  | Weight |  |  |  |  |  |  |  |
|  | Reps |  |  |  |  |  |  |  |
|  | Weight |  |  |  |  |  |  |  |
|  | Reps |  |  |  |  |  |  |  |
|  | Weight |  |  |  |  |  |  |  |
|  | Reps |  |  |  |  |  |  |  |
|  | Weight |  |  |  |  |  |  |  |
|  | Reps |  |  |  |  |  |  |  |
|  | Weight |  |  |  |  |  |  |  |
|  | Reps |  |  |  |  |  |  |  |
|  | Weight |  |  |  |  |  |  |  |

| Cardio | Time | Distance | Heart Rate | Cals Burned |
|---|---|---|---|---|
|  |  |  |  |  |
|  |  |  |  |  |
|  |  |  |  |  |

## Measurements

| Neck | R Bicep | L Bicep | Chest | Waist | Hips | R Thigh | L Thigh | Calf |
|---|---|---|---|---|---|---|---|---|
|  |  |  |  |  |  |  |  |  |
|  |  |  |  |  |  |  |  |  |
|  |  |  |  |  |  |  |  |  |

**Date:** _____  **Muscle Group:** _____

S ○  M ○  T ○  W ○  T ○  F ○  S ○   **Start Time** _____

**Weight:** _____  **Finish Time** _____

☐ **Upper Body**   ☐ **Lower Body**   ☐ **Abs**

| Exercise | Set | 1 | 2 | 3 | 4 | 5 | 6 | 7 |
|---|---|---|---|---|---|---|---|---|
| | Reps | | | | | | | |
| | Weight | | | | | | | |
| | Reps | | | | | | | |
| | Weight | | | | | | | |
| | Reps | | | | | | | |
| | Weight | | | | | | | |
| | Reps | | | | | | | |
| | Weight | | | | | | | |
| | Reps | | | | | | | |
| | Weight | | | | | | | |
| | Reps | | | | | | | |
| | Weight | | | | | | | |
| | Reps | | | | | | | |
| | Weight | | | | | | | |
| | Reps | | | | | | | |
| | Weight | | | | | | | |

| Cardio | Time | Distance | Heart Rate | Cals Burned |
|---|---|---|---|---|
| | | | | |
| | | | | |
| | | | | |

### Measurements

| Neck | R Bicep | L Bicep | Chest | Waist | Hips | R Thigh | L Thigh | Calf |
|---|---|---|---|---|---|---|---|---|
| | | | | | | | | |
| | | | | | | | | |
| | | | | | | | | |

Date: _____  **Muscle Group:** _____

S M T W T F S  **Start Time** _____
○ ○ ○ ○ ○ ○ ○

**Weight:** _____  **Finish Time** _____

☐ Upper Body   ☐ Lower Body   ☐ Abs

| Exercise | Set | 1 | 2 | 3 | 4 | 5 | 6 | 7 |
|---|---|---|---|---|---|---|---|---|
|  | Reps |  |  |  |  |  |  |  |
|  | Weight |  |  |  |  |  |  |  |
|  | Reps |  |  |  |  |  |  |  |
|  | Weight |  |  |  |  |  |  |  |
|  | Reps |  |  |  |  |  |  |  |
|  | Weight |  |  |  |  |  |  |  |
|  | Reps |  |  |  |  |  |  |  |
|  | Weight |  |  |  |  |  |  |  |
|  | Reps |  |  |  |  |  |  |  |
|  | Weight |  |  |  |  |  |  |  |
|  | Reps |  |  |  |  |  |  |  |
|  | Weight |  |  |  |  |  |  |  |
|  | Reps |  |  |  |  |  |  |  |
|  | Weight |  |  |  |  |  |  |  |
|  | Reps |  |  |  |  |  |  |  |
|  | Weight |  |  |  |  |  |  |  |

| Cardio | Time | Distance | Heart Rate | Cals Burned |
|---|---|---|---|---|
|  |  |  |  |  |
|  |  |  |  |  |
|  |  |  |  |  |

### Measurements

| Neck | R Bicep | L Bicep | Chest | Waist | Hips | R Thigh | L Thigh | Calf |
|---|---|---|---|---|---|---|---|---|
|  |  |  |  |  |  |  |  |  |
|  |  |  |  |  |  |  |  |  |
|  |  |  |  |  |  |  |  |  |

Date:_____  Muscle Group: _____

S M T W T F S  Start Time_____
○ ○ ○ ○ ○ ○ ○

Weight:_____  Finish Time_____

☐ Upper Body    ☐ Lower Body    ☐ Abs

| Exercise | Set | 1 | 2 | 3 | 4 | 5 | 6 | 7 |
|---|---|---|---|---|---|---|---|---|
|  | Reps |  |  |  |  |  |  |  |
|  | Weight |  |  |  |  |  |  |  |
|  | Reps |  |  |  |  |  |  |  |
|  | Weight |  |  |  |  |  |  |  |
|  | Reps |  |  |  |  |  |  |  |
|  | Weight |  |  |  |  |  |  |  |
|  | Reps |  |  |  |  |  |  |  |
|  | Weight |  |  |  |  |  |  |  |
|  | Reps |  |  |  |  |  |  |  |
|  | Weight |  |  |  |  |  |  |  |
|  | Reps |  |  |  |  |  |  |  |
|  | Weight |  |  |  |  |  |  |  |
|  | Reps |  |  |  |  |  |  |  |
|  | Weight |  |  |  |  |  |  |  |
|  | Reps |  |  |  |  |  |  |  |
|  | Weight |  |  |  |  |  |  |  |

| Cardio | Time | Distance | Heart Rate | Cals Burned |
|---|---|---|---|---|
|  |  |  |  |  |
|  |  |  |  |  |
|  |  |  |  |  |

## Measurements

| Neck | R Bicep | L Bicep | Chest | Waist | Hips | R Thigh | L Thigh | Calf |
|---|---|---|---|---|---|---|---|---|
|  |  |  |  |  |  |  |  |  |
|  |  |  |  |  |  |  |  |  |
|  |  |  |  |  |  |  |  |  |

Date:_____ Muscle Group: _____

S  M  T  W  T  F  S  Start Time_____
○  ○  ○  ○  ○  ○  ○

Weight:_____ Finish Time_____

☐ Upper Body    ☐ Lower Body    ☐ Abs

| Exercise | Set | 1 | 2 | 3 | 4 | 5 | 6 | 7 |
|---|---|---|---|---|---|---|---|---|
|  | Reps |  |  |  |  |  |  |  |
|  | Weight |  |  |  |  |  |  |  |
|  | Reps |  |  |  |  |  |  |  |
|  | Weight |  |  |  |  |  |  |  |
|  | Reps |  |  |  |  |  |  |  |
|  | Weight |  |  |  |  |  |  |  |
|  | Reps |  |  |  |  |  |  |  |
|  | Weight |  |  |  |  |  |  |  |
|  | Reps |  |  |  |  |  |  |  |
|  | Weight |  |  |  |  |  |  |  |
|  | Reps |  |  |  |  |  |  |  |
|  | Weight |  |  |  |  |  |  |  |
|  | Reps |  |  |  |  |  |  |  |
|  | Weight |  |  |  |  |  |  |  |
|  | Reps |  |  |  |  |  |  |  |
|  | Weight |  |  |  |  |  |  |  |

| Cardio | Time | Distance | Heart Rate | Cals Burned |
|---|---|---|---|---|
|  |  |  |  |  |
|  |  |  |  |  |
|  |  |  |  |  |

## Measurements

| Neck | R Bicep | L Bicep | Chest | Waist | Hips | R Thigh | L Thigh | Calf |
|---|---|---|---|---|---|---|---|---|
|  |  |  |  |  |  |  |  |  |
|  |  |  |  |  |  |  |  |  |
|  |  |  |  |  |  |  |  |  |

**Date:** _____  **Muscle Group:** _____

S  M  T  W  T  F  S   **Start Time** _____
○  ○  ○  ○  ○  ○  ○

**Weight:** _____  **Finish Time** _____

☐ **Upper Body**   ☐ **Lower Body**   ☐ **Abs**

| Exercise | Set | 1 | 2 | 3 | 4 | 5 | 6 | 7 |
|---|---|---|---|---|---|---|---|---|
|  | Reps |  |  |  |  |  |  |  |
|  | Weight |  |  |  |  |  |  |  |
|  | Reps |  |  |  |  |  |  |  |
|  | Weight |  |  |  |  |  |  |  |
|  | Reps |  |  |  |  |  |  |  |
|  | Weight |  |  |  |  |  |  |  |
|  | Reps |  |  |  |  |  |  |  |
|  | Weight |  |  |  |  |  |  |  |
|  | Reps |  |  |  |  |  |  |  |
|  | Weight |  |  |  |  |  |  |  |
|  | Reps |  |  |  |  |  |  |  |
|  | Weight |  |  |  |  |  |  |  |
|  | Reps |  |  |  |  |  |  |  |
|  | Weight |  |  |  |  |  |  |  |
|  | Reps |  |  |  |  |  |  |  |
|  | Weight |  |  |  |  |  |  |  |

| Cardio | Time | Distance | Heart Rate | Cals Burned |
|---|---|---|---|---|
|  |  |  |  |  |
|  |  |  |  |  |
|  |  |  |  |  |

### Measurements

| Neck | R Bicep | L Bicep | Chest | Waist | Hips | R Thigh | L Thigh | Calf |
|---|---|---|---|---|---|---|---|---|
|  |  |  |  |  |  |  |  |  |
|  |  |  |  |  |  |  |  |  |
|  |  |  |  |  |  |  |  |  |

**Date:** _____  **Muscle Group:** _____

S  M  T  W  T  F  S  **Start Time** _____
○  ○  ○  ○  ○  ○  ○

**Weight:** _____  **Finish Time** _____

☐ Upper Body    ☐ Lower Body    ☐ Abs

| Exercise | Set | 1 | 2 | 3 | 4 | 5 | 6 | 7 |
|---|---|---|---|---|---|---|---|---|
|  | Reps |  |  |  |  |  |  |  |
|  | Weight |  |  |  |  |  |  |  |
|  | Reps |  |  |  |  |  |  |  |
|  | Weight |  |  |  |  |  |  |  |
|  | Reps |  |  |  |  |  |  |  |
|  | Weight |  |  |  |  |  |  |  |
|  | Reps |  |  |  |  |  |  |  |
|  | Weight |  |  |  |  |  |  |  |
|  | Reps |  |  |  |  |  |  |  |
|  | Weight |  |  |  |  |  |  |  |
|  | Reps |  |  |  |  |  |  |  |
|  | Weight |  |  |  |  |  |  |  |
|  | Reps |  |  |  |  |  |  |  |
|  | Weight |  |  |  |  |  |  |  |
|  | Reps |  |  |  |  |  |  |  |
|  | Weight |  |  |  |  |  |  |  |

| Cardio | Time | Distance | Heart Rate | Cals Burned |
|---|---|---|---|---|
|  |  |  |  |  |
|  |  |  |  |  |
|  |  |  |  |  |

## Measurements

| Neck | R Bicep | L Bicep | Chest | Waist | Hips | R Thigh | L Thigh | Calf |
|---|---|---|---|---|---|---|---|---|
|  |  |  |  |  |  |  |  |  |
|  |  |  |  |  |  |  |  |  |
|  |  |  |  |  |  |  |  |  |

Date:_____  Muscle Group: _____

S M T W T F S  Start Time _____
○ ○ ○ ○ ○ ○ ○

Weight:_____  Finish Time _____

☐ Upper Body   ☐ Lower Body   ☐ Abs

| Exercise | Set | 1 | 2 | 3 | 4 | 5 | 6 | 7 |
|---|---|---|---|---|---|---|---|---|
|  | Reps |  |  |  |  |  |  |  |
|  | Weight |  |  |  |  |  |  |  |
|  | Reps |  |  |  |  |  |  |  |
|  | Weight |  |  |  |  |  |  |  |
|  | Reps |  |  |  |  |  |  |  |
|  | Weight |  |  |  |  |  |  |  |
|  | Reps |  |  |  |  |  |  |  |
|  | Weight |  |  |  |  |  |  |  |
|  | Reps |  |  |  |  |  |  |  |
|  | Weight |  |  |  |  |  |  |  |
|  | Reps |  |  |  |  |  |  |  |
|  | Weight |  |  |  |  |  |  |  |
|  | Reps |  |  |  |  |  |  |  |
|  | Weight |  |  |  |  |  |  |  |
|  | Reps |  |  |  |  |  |  |  |
|  | Weight |  |  |  |  |  |  |  |

| Cardio | Time | Distance | Heart Rate | Cals Burned |
|---|---|---|---|---|
|  |  |  |  |  |
|  |  |  |  |  |
|  |  |  |  |  |

### Measurements

| Neck | R Bicep | L Bicep | Chest | Waist | Hips | R Thigh | L Thigh | Calf |
|---|---|---|---|---|---|---|---|---|
|  |  |  |  |  |  |  |  |  |
|  |  |  |  |  |  |  |  |  |
|  |  |  |  |  |  |  |  |  |

**Date:** _____  **Muscle Group:** _____

S  M  T  W  T  F  S   **Start Time** _____
○  ○  ○  ○  ○  ○  ○

**Weight:** _____  **Finish Time** _____

☐ **Upper Body**    ☐ **Lower Body**    ☐ **Abs**

| Exercise | Set | 1 | 2 | 3 | 4 | 5 | 6 | 7 |
|---|---|---|---|---|---|---|---|---|
|  | Reps |  |  |  |  |  |  |  |
|  | Weight |  |  |  |  |  |  |  |
|  | Reps |  |  |  |  |  |  |  |
|  | Weight |  |  |  |  |  |  |  |
|  | Reps |  |  |  |  |  |  |  |
|  | Weight |  |  |  |  |  |  |  |
|  | Reps |  |  |  |  |  |  |  |
|  | Weight |  |  |  |  |  |  |  |
|  | Reps |  |  |  |  |  |  |  |
|  | Weight |  |  |  |  |  |  |  |
|  | Reps |  |  |  |  |  |  |  |
|  | Weight |  |  |  |  |  |  |  |
|  | Reps |  |  |  |  |  |  |  |
|  | Weight |  |  |  |  |  |  |  |
|  | Reps |  |  |  |  |  |  |  |
|  | Weight |  |  |  |  |  |  |  |

| Cardio | Time | Distance | Heart Rate | Cals Burned |
|---|---|---|---|---|
|  |  |  |  |  |
|  |  |  |  |  |
|  |  |  |  |  |

### Measurements

| Neck | R Bicep | L Bicep | Chest | Waist | Hips | R Thigh | L Thigh | Calf |
|---|---|---|---|---|---|---|---|---|
|  |  |  |  |  |  |  |  |  |
|  |  |  |  |  |  |  |  |  |
|  |  |  |  |  |  |  |  |  |

**Date:** _____  **Muscle Group:** _____

S   M   T   W   T   F   S
○   ○   ○   ○   ○   ○   ○   **Start Time** _____

**Weight:** _____  **Finish Time** _____

☐ Upper Body          ☐ Lower Body          ☐ Abs

| Exercise | Set | 1 | 2 | 3 | 4 | 5 | 6 | 7 |
|---|---|---|---|---|---|---|---|---|
|  | Reps |  |  |  |  |  |  |  |
|  | Weight |  |  |  |  |  |  |  |
|  | Reps |  |  |  |  |  |  |  |
|  | Weight |  |  |  |  |  |  |  |
|  | Reps |  |  |  |  |  |  |  |
|  | Weight |  |  |  |  |  |  |  |
|  | Reps |  |  |  |  |  |  |  |
|  | Weight |  |  |  |  |  |  |  |
|  | Reps |  |  |  |  |  |  |  |
|  | Weight |  |  |  |  |  |  |  |
|  | Reps |  |  |  |  |  |  |  |
|  | Weight |  |  |  |  |  |  |  |
|  | Reps |  |  |  |  |  |  |  |
|  | Weight |  |  |  |  |  |  |  |
|  | Reps |  |  |  |  |  |  |  |
|  | Weight |  |  |  |  |  |  |  |

| Cardio | Time | Distance | Heart Rate | Cals Burned |
|---|---|---|---|---|
|  |  |  |  |  |
|  |  |  |  |  |
|  |  |  |  |  |

### Measurements

| Neck | R Bicep | L Bicep | Chest | Waist | Hips | R Thigh | L Thigh | Calf |
|---|---|---|---|---|---|---|---|---|
|  |  |  |  |  |  |  |  |  |
|  |  |  |  |  |  |  |  |  |
|  |  |  |  |  |  |  |  |  |

**Date:** _____  **Muscle Group:** _____

S  M  T  W  T  F  S   **Start Time** _____
○  ○  ○  ○  ○  ○  ○

**Weight:** _____  **Finish Time** _____

☐ Upper Body     ☐ Lower Body     ☐ Abs

| Exercise | Set | 1 | 2 | 3 | 4 | 5 | 6 | 7 |
|---|---|---|---|---|---|---|---|---|
|  | Reps |  |  |  |  |  |  |  |
|  | Weight |  |  |  |  |  |  |  |
|  | Reps |  |  |  |  |  |  |  |
|  | Weight |  |  |  |  |  |  |  |
|  | Reps |  |  |  |  |  |  |  |
|  | Weight |  |  |  |  |  |  |  |
|  | Reps |  |  |  |  |  |  |  |
|  | Weight |  |  |  |  |  |  |  |
|  | Reps |  |  |  |  |  |  |  |
|  | Weight |  |  |  |  |  |  |  |
|  | Reps |  |  |  |  |  |  |  |
|  | Weight |  |  |  |  |  |  |  |
|  | Reps |  |  |  |  |  |  |  |
|  | Weight |  |  |  |  |  |  |  |
|  | Reps |  |  |  |  |  |  |  |
|  | Weight |  |  |  |  |  |  |  |

| Cardio | Time | Distance | Heart Rate | Cals Burned |
|---|---|---|---|---|
|  |  |  |  |  |
|  |  |  |  |  |
|  |  |  |  |  |

## Measurements

| Neck | R Bicep | L Bicep | Chest | Waist | Hips | R Thigh | L Thigh | Calf |
|---|---|---|---|---|---|---|---|---|
|  |  |  |  |  |  |  |  |  |
|  |  |  |  |  |  |  |  |  |
|  |  |  |  |  |  |  |  |  |

**Date:** _____  **Muscle Group:** _____

S M T W T F S   **Start Time** _____
○ ○ ○ ○ ○ ○ ○

**Weight:** _____  **Finish Time** _____

☐ Upper Body   ☐ Lower Body   ☐ Abs

| Exercise | Set | 1 | 2 | 3 | 4 | 5 | 6 | 7 |
|---|---|---|---|---|---|---|---|---|
|  | Reps |  |  |  |  |  |  |  |
|  | Weight |  |  |  |  |  |  |  |
|  | Reps |  |  |  |  |  |  |  |
|  | Weight |  |  |  |  |  |  |  |
|  | Reps |  |  |  |  |  |  |  |
|  | Weight |  |  |  |  |  |  |  |
|  | Reps |  |  |  |  |  |  |  |
|  | Weight |  |  |  |  |  |  |  |
|  | Reps |  |  |  |  |  |  |  |
|  | Weight |  |  |  |  |  |  |  |
|  | Reps |  |  |  |  |  |  |  |
|  | Weight |  |  |  |  |  |  |  |
|  | Reps |  |  |  |  |  |  |  |
|  | Weight |  |  |  |  |  |  |  |
|  | Reps |  |  |  |  |  |  |  |
|  | Weight |  |  |  |  |  |  |  |

| Cardio | Time | Distance | Heart Rate | Cals Burned |
|---|---|---|---|---|
|  |  |  |  |  |
|  |  |  |  |  |
|  |  |  |  |  |

### Measurements

| Neck | R Bicep | L Bicep | Chest | Waist | Hips | R Thigh | L Thigh | Calf |
|---|---|---|---|---|---|---|---|---|
|  |  |  |  |  |  |  |  |  |
|  |  |  |  |  |  |  |  |  |
|  |  |  |  |  |  |  |  |  |

**Date:** _____     **Muscle Group:** _____

S  M  T  W  T  F  S     **Start Time** _____
○  ○  ○  ○  ○  ○  ○

**Weight:** _____     **Finish Time** _____

☐ **Upper Body**     ☐ **Lower Body**     ☐ **Abs**

| Exercise | Set | 1 | 2 | 3 | 4 | 5 | 6 | 7 |
|---|---|---|---|---|---|---|---|---|
| | Reps | | | | | | | |
| | Weight | | | | | | | |
| | Reps | | | | | | | |
| | Weight | | | | | | | |
| | Reps | | | | | | | |
| | Weight | | | | | | | |
| | Reps | | | | | | | |
| | Weight | | | | | | | |
| | Reps | | | | | | | |
| | Weight | | | | | | | |
| | Reps | | | | | | | |
| | Weight | | | | | | | |
| | Reps | | | | | | | |
| | Weight | | | | | | | |
| | Reps | | | | | | | |
| | Weight | | | | | | | |

| Cardio | Time | Distance | Heart Rate | Cals Burned |
|---|---|---|---|---|
| | | | | |
| | | | | |
| | | | | |

## Measurements

| Neck | R Bicep | L Bicep | Chest | Waist | Hips | R Thigh | L Thigh | Calf |
|---|---|---|---|---|---|---|---|---|
| | | | | | | | | |
| | | | | | | | | |
| | | | | | | | | |

Date:_____ Muscle Group:_____

S M T W T F S  Start Time_____
○ ○ ○ ○ ○ ○ ○

Weight:_____ Finish Time_____

☐ Upper Body  ☐ Lower Body  ☐ Abs

| Exercise | Set | 1 | 2 | 3 | 4 | 5 | 6 | 7 |
|---|---|---|---|---|---|---|---|---|
|  | Reps |  |  |  |  |  |  |  |
|  | Weight |  |  |  |  |  |  |  |
|  | Reps |  |  |  |  |  |  |  |
|  | Weight |  |  |  |  |  |  |  |
|  | Reps |  |  |  |  |  |  |  |
|  | Weight |  |  |  |  |  |  |  |
|  | Reps |  |  |  |  |  |  |  |
|  | Weight |  |  |  |  |  |  |  |
|  | Reps |  |  |  |  |  |  |  |
|  | Weight |  |  |  |  |  |  |  |
|  | Reps |  |  |  |  |  |  |  |
|  | Weight |  |  |  |  |  |  |  |
|  | Reps |  |  |  |  |  |  |  |
|  | Weight |  |  |  |  |  |  |  |
|  | Reps |  |  |  |  |  |  |  |
|  | Weight |  |  |  |  |  |  |  |

| Cardio | Time | Distance | Heart Rate | Cals Burned |
|---|---|---|---|---|
|  |  |  |  |  |
|  |  |  |  |  |
|  |  |  |  |  |

## Measurements

| Neck | R Bicep | L Bicep | Chest | Waist | Hips | R Thigh | L Thigh | Calf |
|---|---|---|---|---|---|---|---|---|
|  |  |  |  |  |  |  |  |  |
|  |  |  |  |  |  |  |  |  |
|  |  |  |  |  |  |  |  |  |

**Date:**_____ **Muscle Group:** _____

S M T W T F S  **Start Time**_____
○ ○ ○ ○ ○ ○ ○

**Weight:**_____ **Finish Time**_____

☐ Upper Body   ☐ Lower Body   ☐ Abs

| Exercise | Set | 1 | 2 | 3 | 4 | 5 | 6 | 7 |
|---|---|---|---|---|---|---|---|---|
|  | Reps |  |  |  |  |  |  |  |
|  | Weight |  |  |  |  |  |  |  |
|  | Reps |  |  |  |  |  |  |  |
|  | Weight |  |  |  |  |  |  |  |
|  | Reps |  |  |  |  |  |  |  |
|  | Weight |  |  |  |  |  |  |  |
|  | Reps |  |  |  |  |  |  |  |
|  | Weight |  |  |  |  |  |  |  |
|  | Reps |  |  |  |  |  |  |  |
|  | Weight |  |  |  |  |  |  |  |
|  | Reps |  |  |  |  |  |  |  |
|  | Weight |  |  |  |  |  |  |  |
|  | Reps |  |  |  |  |  |  |  |
|  | Weight |  |  |  |  |  |  |  |
|  | Reps |  |  |  |  |  |  |  |
|  | Weight |  |  |  |  |  |  |  |

| Cardio | Time | Distance | Heart Rate | Cals Burned |
|---|---|---|---|---|
|  |  |  |  |  |
|  |  |  |  |  |
|  |  |  |  |  |

## Measurements

| Neck | R Bicep | L Bicep | Chest | Waist | Hips | R Thigh | L Thigh | Calf |
|---|---|---|---|---|---|---|---|---|
|  |  |  |  |  |  |  |  |  |
|  |  |  |  |  |  |  |  |  |
|  |  |  |  |  |  |  |  |  |

Date:_____ Muscle Group:_____

S M T W T F S  Start Time_____
○ ○ ○ ○ ○ ○ ○

Weight:_____ Finish Time_____

☐ Upper Body   ☐ Lower Body   ☐ Abs

| Exercise | Set | 1 | 2 | 3 | 4 | 5 | 6 | 7 |
|---|---|---|---|---|---|---|---|---|
|  | Reps |  |  |  |  |  |  |  |
|  | Weight |  |  |  |  |  |  |  |
|  | Reps |  |  |  |  |  |  |  |
|  | Weight |  |  |  |  |  |  |  |
|  | Reps |  |  |  |  |  |  |  |
|  | Weight |  |  |  |  |  |  |  |
|  | Reps |  |  |  |  |  |  |  |
|  | Weight |  |  |  |  |  |  |  |
|  | Reps |  |  |  |  |  |  |  |
|  | Weight |  |  |  |  |  |  |  |
|  | Reps |  |  |  |  |  |  |  |
|  | Weight |  |  |  |  |  |  |  |
|  | Reps |  |  |  |  |  |  |  |
|  | Weight |  |  |  |  |  |  |  |
|  | Reps |  |  |  |  |  |  |  |
|  | Weight |  |  |  |  |  |  |  |

| Cardio | Time | Distance | Heart Rate | Cals Burned |
|---|---|---|---|---|
|  |  |  |  |  |
|  |  |  |  |  |
|  |  |  |  |  |

## Measurements

| Neck | R Bicep | L Bicep | Chest | Waist | Hips | R Thigh | L Thigh | Calf |
|---|---|---|---|---|---|---|---|---|
|  |  |  |  |  |  |  |  |  |
|  |  |  |  |  |  |  |  |  |
|  |  |  |  |  |  |  |  |  |

**Date:** _____  **Muscle Group:** _____

S  M  T  W  T  F  S   **Start Time** _____
○  ○  ○  ○  ○  ○  ○

**Weight:** _____  **Finish Time** _____

☐ **Upper Body**   ☐ **Lower Body**   ☐ **Abs**

| Exercise | Set | 1 | 2 | 3 | 4 | 5 | 6 | 7 |
|---|---|---|---|---|---|---|---|---|
|  | Reps |  |  |  |  |  |  |  |
|  | Weight |  |  |  |  |  |  |  |
|  | Reps |  |  |  |  |  |  |  |
|  | Weight |  |  |  |  |  |  |  |
|  | Reps |  |  |  |  |  |  |  |
|  | Weight |  |  |  |  |  |  |  |
|  | Reps |  |  |  |  |  |  |  |
|  | Weight |  |  |  |  |  |  |  |
|  | Reps |  |  |  |  |  |  |  |
|  | Weight |  |  |  |  |  |  |  |
|  | Reps |  |  |  |  |  |  |  |
|  | Weight |  |  |  |  |  |  |  |
|  | Reps |  |  |  |  |  |  |  |
|  | Weight |  |  |  |  |  |  |  |
|  | Reps |  |  |  |  |  |  |  |
|  | Weight |  |  |  |  |  |  |  |

| Cardio | Time | Distance | Heart Rate | Cals Burned |
|---|---|---|---|---|
|  |  |  |  |  |
|  |  |  |  |  |
|  |  |  |  |  |

## Measurements

| Neck | R Bicep | L Bicep | Chest | Waist | Hips | R Thigh | L Thigh | Calf |
|---|---|---|---|---|---|---|---|---|
|  |  |  |  |  |  |  |  |  |
|  |  |  |  |  |  |  |  |  |
|  |  |  |  |  |  |  |  |  |

**Date:** _____  **Muscle Group:** _____

S  M  T  W  T  F  S  **Start Time** _____
○  ○  ○  ○  ○  ○  ○

**Weight:** _____  **Finish Time** _____

☐ Upper Body     ☐ Lower Body     ☐ Abs

| Exercise | Set | 1 | 2 | 3 | 4 | 5 | 6 | 7 |
|---|---|---|---|---|---|---|---|---|
|  | Reps |  |  |  |  |  |  |  |
|  | Weight |  |  |  |  |  |  |  |
|  | Reps |  |  |  |  |  |  |  |
|  | Weight |  |  |  |  |  |  |  |
|  | Reps |  |  |  |  |  |  |  |
|  | Weight |  |  |  |  |  |  |  |
|  | Reps |  |  |  |  |  |  |  |
|  | Weight |  |  |  |  |  |  |  |
|  | Reps |  |  |  |  |  |  |  |
|  | Weight |  |  |  |  |  |  |  |
|  | Reps |  |  |  |  |  |  |  |
|  | Weight |  |  |  |  |  |  |  |
|  | Reps |  |  |  |  |  |  |  |
|  | Weight |  |  |  |  |  |  |  |
|  | Reps |  |  |  |  |  |  |  |
|  | Weight |  |  |  |  |  |  |  |

| Cardio | Time | Distance | Heart Rate | Cals Burned |
|---|---|---|---|---|
|  |  |  |  |  |
|  |  |  |  |  |
|  |  |  |  |  |

## Measurements

| Neck | R Bicep | L Bicep | Chest | Waist | Hips | R Thigh | L Thigh | Calf |
|---|---|---|---|---|---|---|---|---|
|  |  |  |  |  |  |  |  |  |
|  |  |  |  |  |  |  |  |  |
|  |  |  |  |  |  |  |  |  |

Date: _____ Muscle Group: _____

S M T W T F S  Start Time _____
○ ○ ○ ○ ○ ○ ○

Weight: _____ Finish Time _____

☐ Upper Body  ☐ Lower Body  ☐ Abs

| Exercise | Set | 1 | 2 | 3 | 4 | 5 | 6 | 7 |
|---|---|---|---|---|---|---|---|---|
|  | Reps |  |  |  |  |  |  |  |
|  | Weight |  |  |  |  |  |  |  |
|  | Reps |  |  |  |  |  |  |  |
|  | Weight |  |  |  |  |  |  |  |
|  | Reps |  |  |  |  |  |  |  |
|  | Weight |  |  |  |  |  |  |  |
|  | Reps |  |  |  |  |  |  |  |
|  | Weight |  |  |  |  |  |  |  |
|  | Reps |  |  |  |  |  |  |  |
|  | Weight |  |  |  |  |  |  |  |
|  | Reps |  |  |  |  |  |  |  |
|  | Weight |  |  |  |  |  |  |  |
|  | Reps |  |  |  |  |  |  |  |
|  | Weight |  |  |  |  |  |  |  |
|  | Reps |  |  |  |  |  |  |  |
|  | Weight |  |  |  |  |  |  |  |

| Cardio | Time | Distance | Heart Rate | Cals Burned |
|---|---|---|---|---|
|  |  |  |  |  |
|  |  |  |  |  |
|  |  |  |  |  |

## Measurements

| Neck | R Bicep | L Bicep | Chest | Waist | Hips | R Thigh | L Thigh | Calf |
|---|---|---|---|---|---|---|---|---|
|  |  |  |  |  |  |  |  |  |
|  |  |  |  |  |  |  |  |  |
|  |  |  |  |  |  |  |  |  |

**Date:** _____  **Muscle Group:** _____

S  M  T  W  T  F  S
○  ○  ○  ○  ○  ○  ○    **Start Time** _____

**Weight:** _____    **Finish Time** _____

☐ Upper Body    ☐ Lower Body    ☐ Abs

| Exercise | Set | 1 | 2 | 3 | 4 | 5 | 6 | 7 |
|---|---|---|---|---|---|---|---|---|
|  | Reps |  |  |  |  |  |  |  |
|  | Weight |  |  |  |  |  |  |  |
|  | Reps |  |  |  |  |  |  |  |
|  | Weight |  |  |  |  |  |  |  |
|  | Reps |  |  |  |  |  |  |  |
|  | Weight |  |  |  |  |  |  |  |
|  | Reps |  |  |  |  |  |  |  |
|  | Weight |  |  |  |  |  |  |  |
|  | Reps |  |  |  |  |  |  |  |
|  | Weight |  |  |  |  |  |  |  |
|  | Reps |  |  |  |  |  |  |  |
|  | Weight |  |  |  |  |  |  |  |
|  | Reps |  |  |  |  |  |  |  |
|  | Weight |  |  |  |  |  |  |  |
|  | Reps |  |  |  |  |  |  |  |
|  | Weight |  |  |  |  |  |  |  |

| Cardio | Time | Distance | Heart Rate | Cals Burned |
|---|---|---|---|---|
|  |  |  |  |  |
|  |  |  |  |  |
|  |  |  |  |  |

### Measurements

| Neck | R Bicep | L Bicep | Chest | Waist | Hips | R Thigh | L Thigh | Calf |
|---|---|---|---|---|---|---|---|---|
|  |  |  |  |  |  |  |  |  |
|  |  |  |  |  |  |  |  |  |
|  |  |  |  |  |  |  |  |  |

**Date:** _____  **Muscle Group:** _____

S   M   T   W   T   F   S   **Start Time** _____
○   ○   ○   ○   ○   ○   ○

**Weight:** _____  **Finish Time** _____

☐ Upper Body     ☐ Lower Body     ☐ Abs

| Exercise | Set | 1 | 2 | 3 | 4 | 5 | 6 | 7 |
|---|---|---|---|---|---|---|---|---|
|  | Reps |  |  |  |  |  |  |  |
|  | Weight |  |  |  |  |  |  |  |
|  | Reps |  |  |  |  |  |  |  |
|  | Weight |  |  |  |  |  |  |  |
|  | Reps |  |  |  |  |  |  |  |
|  | Weight |  |  |  |  |  |  |  |
|  | Reps |  |  |  |  |  |  |  |
|  | Weight |  |  |  |  |  |  |  |
|  | Reps |  |  |  |  |  |  |  |
|  | Weight |  |  |  |  |  |  |  |
|  | Reps |  |  |  |  |  |  |  |
|  | Weight |  |  |  |  |  |  |  |
|  | Reps |  |  |  |  |  |  |  |
|  | Weight |  |  |  |  |  |  |  |
|  | Reps |  |  |  |  |  |  |  |
|  | Weight |  |  |  |  |  |  |  |

| Cardio | Time | Distance | Heart Rate | Cals Burned |
|---|---|---|---|---|
|  |  |  |  |  |
|  |  |  |  |  |
|  |  |  |  |  |

## Measurements

| Neck | R Bicep | L Bicep | Chest | Waist | Hips | R Thigh | L Thigh | Calf |
|---|---|---|---|---|---|---|---|---|
|  |  |  |  |  |  |  |  |  |
|  |  |  |  |  |  |  |  |  |
|  |  |  |  |  |  |  |  |  |

**Date:** _____  **Muscle Group:** _____

S M T W T F S  **Start Time** _____
○ ○ ○ ○ ○ ○ ○

**Weight:** _____  **Finish Time** _____

☐ **Upper Body**   ☐ **Lower Body**   ☐ **Abs**

| Exercise | Set | 1 | 2 | 3 | 4 | 5 | 6 | 7 |
|---|---|---|---|---|---|---|---|---|
| | Reps | | | | | | | |
| | Weight | | | | | | | |
| | Reps | | | | | | | |
| | Weight | | | | | | | |
| | Reps | | | | | | | |
| | Weight | | | | | | | |
| | Reps | | | | | | | |
| | Weight | | | | | | | |
| | Reps | | | | | | | |
| | Weight | | | | | | | |
| | Reps | | | | | | | |
| | Weight | | | | | | | |
| | Reps | | | | | | | |
| | Weight | | | | | | | |
| | Reps | | | | | | | |
| | Weight | | | | | | | |

| Cardio | Time | Distance | Heart Rate | Cals Burned |
|---|---|---|---|---|
| | | | | |
| | | | | |
| | | | | |

## Measurements

| Neck | R Bicep | L Bicep | Chest | Waist | Hips | R Thigh | L Thigh | Calf |
|---|---|---|---|---|---|---|---|---|
| | | | | | | | | |
| | | | | | | | | |
| | | | | | | | | |

**Date:** _____  **Muscle Group:** _____

S  M  T  W  T  F  S   **Start Time** _____
○  ○  ○  ○  ○  ○  ○

**Weight:** _____  **Finish Time** _____

☐ **Upper Body**   ☐ **Lower Body**   ☐ **Abs**

| Exercise | Set | 1 | 2 | 3 | 4 | 5 | 6 | 7 |
|---|---|---|---|---|---|---|---|---|
|  | Reps |  |  |  |  |  |  |  |
|  | Weight |  |  |  |  |  |  |  |
|  | Reps |  |  |  |  |  |  |  |
|  | Weight |  |  |  |  |  |  |  |
|  | Reps |  |  |  |  |  |  |  |
|  | Weight |  |  |  |  |  |  |  |
|  | Reps |  |  |  |  |  |  |  |
|  | Weight |  |  |  |  |  |  |  |
|  | Reps |  |  |  |  |  |  |  |
|  | Weight |  |  |  |  |  |  |  |
|  | Reps |  |  |  |  |  |  |  |
|  | Weight |  |  |  |  |  |  |  |
|  | Reps |  |  |  |  |  |  |  |
|  | Weight |  |  |  |  |  |  |  |
|  | Reps |  |  |  |  |  |  |  |
|  | Weight |  |  |  |  |  |  |  |

| Cardio | Time | Distance | Heart Rate | Cals Burned |
|---|---|---|---|---|
|  |  |  |  |  |
|  |  |  |  |  |
|  |  |  |  |  |

## Measurements

| Neck | R Bicep | L Bicep | Chest | Waist | Hips | R Thigh | L Thigh | Calf |
|---|---|---|---|---|---|---|---|---|
|  |  |  |  |  |  |  |  |  |
|  |  |  |  |  |  |  |  |  |
|  |  |  |  |  |  |  |  |  |

**Date:** _____   **Muscle Group:** _____

S  M  T  W  T  F  S   **Start Time** _____
○  ○  ○  ○  ○  ○  ○

**Weight:** _____   **Finish Time** _____

☐ **Upper Body**      ☐ **Lower Body**      ☐ **Abs**

| Exercise | Set | 1 | 2 | 3 | 4 | 5 | 6 | 7 |
|---|---|---|---|---|---|---|---|---|
|  | Reps |  |  |  |  |  |  |  |
|  | Weight |  |  |  |  |  |  |  |
|  | Reps |  |  |  |  |  |  |  |
|  | Weight |  |  |  |  |  |  |  |
|  | Reps |  |  |  |  |  |  |  |
|  | Weight |  |  |  |  |  |  |  |
|  | Reps |  |  |  |  |  |  |  |
|  | Weight |  |  |  |  |  |  |  |
|  | Reps |  |  |  |  |  |  |  |
|  | Weight |  |  |  |  |  |  |  |
|  | Reps |  |  |  |  |  |  |  |
|  | Weight |  |  |  |  |  |  |  |
|  | Reps |  |  |  |  |  |  |  |
|  | Weight |  |  |  |  |  |  |  |
|  | Reps |  |  |  |  |  |  |  |
|  | Weight |  |  |  |  |  |  |  |

| Cardio | Time | Distance | Heart Rate | Cals Burned |
|---|---|---|---|---|
|  |  |  |  |  |
|  |  |  |  |  |
|  |  |  |  |  |

### Measurements

| Neck | R Bicep | L Bicep | Chest | Waist | Hips | R Thigh | L Thigh | Calf |
|---|---|---|---|---|---|---|---|---|
|  |  |  |  |  |  |  |  |  |
|  |  |  |  |  |  |  |  |  |
|  |  |  |  |  |  |  |  |  |

**Date:** _____  **Muscle Group:** _____

S  M  T  W  T  F  S  **Start Time** _____
○  ○  ○  ○  ○  ○  ○

**Weight:** _____  **Finish Time** _____

☐ Upper Body   ☐ Lower Body   ☐ Abs

| Exercise | Set | 1 | 2 | 3 | 4 | 5 | 6 | 7 |
|---|---|---|---|---|---|---|---|---|
|  | Reps |  |  |  |  |  |  |  |
|  | Weight |  |  |  |  |  |  |  |
|  | Reps |  |  |  |  |  |  |  |
|  | Weight |  |  |  |  |  |  |  |
|  | Reps |  |  |  |  |  |  |  |
|  | Weight |  |  |  |  |  |  |  |
|  | Reps |  |  |  |  |  |  |  |
|  | Weight |  |  |  |  |  |  |  |
|  | Reps |  |  |  |  |  |  |  |
|  | Weight |  |  |  |  |  |  |  |
|  | Reps |  |  |  |  |  |  |  |
|  | Weight |  |  |  |  |  |  |  |
|  | Reps |  |  |  |  |  |  |  |
|  | Weight |  |  |  |  |  |  |  |
|  | Reps |  |  |  |  |  |  |  |
|  | Weight |  |  |  |  |  |  |  |

| Cardio | Time | Distance | Heart Rate | Cals Burned |
|---|---|---|---|---|
|  |  |  |  |  |
|  |  |  |  |  |
|  |  |  |  |  |

## Measurements

| Neck | R Bicep | L Bicep | Chest | Waist | Hips | R Thigh | L Thigh | Calf |
|---|---|---|---|---|---|---|---|---|
|  |  |  |  |  |  |  |  |  |
|  |  |  |  |  |  |  |  |  |
|  |  |  |  |  |  |  |  |  |

**Date:** _____    **Muscle Group:** _____

S   M   T   W   T   F   S    **Start Time** _____
○   ○   ○   ○   ○   ○   ○

**Weight:** _____    **Finish Time** _____

☐ **Upper Body**     ☐ **Lower Body**     ☐ **Abs**

| Exercise | Set | 1 | 2 | 3 | 4 | 5 | 6 | 7 |
|---|---|---|---|---|---|---|---|---|
|  | Reps |  |  |  |  |  |  |  |
|  | Weight |  |  |  |  |  |  |  |
|  | Reps |  |  |  |  |  |  |  |
|  | Weight |  |  |  |  |  |  |  |
|  | Reps |  |  |  |  |  |  |  |
|  | Weight |  |  |  |  |  |  |  |
|  | Reps |  |  |  |  |  |  |  |
|  | Weight |  |  |  |  |  |  |  |
|  | Reps |  |  |  |  |  |  |  |
|  | Weight |  |  |  |  |  |  |  |
|  | Reps |  |  |  |  |  |  |  |
|  | Weight |  |  |  |  |  |  |  |
|  | Reps |  |  |  |  |  |  |  |
|  | Weight |  |  |  |  |  |  |  |
|  | Reps |  |  |  |  |  |  |  |
|  | Weight |  |  |  |  |  |  |  |

| Cardio | Time | Distance | Heart Rate | Cals Burned |
|---|---|---|---|---|
|  |  |  |  |  |
|  |  |  |  |  |
|  |  |  |  |  |

## Measurements

| Neck | R Bicep | L Bicep | Chest | Waist | Hips | R Thigh | L Thigh | Calf |
|---|---|---|---|---|---|---|---|---|
|  |  |  |  |  |  |  |  |  |
|  |  |  |  |  |  |  |  |  |
|  |  |  |  |  |  |  |  |  |

**Date:** _____  **Muscle Group:** _____

S  M  T  W  T  F  S   **Start Time** _____
○  ○  ○  ○  ○  ○  ○

**Weight:** _____  **Finish Time** _____

☐ Upper Body     ☐ Lower Body     ☐ Abs

| Exercise | Set | 1 | 2 | 3 | 4 | 5 | 6 | 7 |
|---|---|---|---|---|---|---|---|---|
|  | Reps |  |  |  |  |  |  |  |
|  | Weight |  |  |  |  |  |  |  |
|  | Reps |  |  |  |  |  |  |  |
|  | Weight |  |  |  |  |  |  |  |
|  | Reps |  |  |  |  |  |  |  |
|  | Weight |  |  |  |  |  |  |  |
|  | Reps |  |  |  |  |  |  |  |
|  | Weight |  |  |  |  |  |  |  |
|  | Reps |  |  |  |  |  |  |  |
|  | Weight |  |  |  |  |  |  |  |
|  | Reps |  |  |  |  |  |  |  |
|  | Weight |  |  |  |  |  |  |  |
|  | Reps |  |  |  |  |  |  |  |
|  | Weight |  |  |  |  |  |  |  |
|  | Reps |  |  |  |  |  |  |  |
|  | Weight |  |  |  |  |  |  |  |

| Cardio | Time | Distance | Heart Rate | Cals Burned |
|---|---|---|---|---|
|  |  |  |  |  |
|  |  |  |  |  |
|  |  |  |  |  |

## Measurements

| Neck | R Bicep | L Bicep | Chest | Waist | Hips | R Thigh | L Thigh | Calf |
|---|---|---|---|---|---|---|---|---|
|  |  |  |  |  |  |  |  |  |
|  |  |  |  |  |  |  |  |  |
|  |  |  |  |  |  |  |  |  |

**Date:** _____  **Muscle Group:** _____

S M T W T F S   **Start Time** _____
○ ○ ○ ○ ○ ○ ○

**Weight:** _____  **Finish Time** _____

☐ **Upper Body**   ☐ **Lower Body**   ☐ **Abs**

| Exercise | Set | 1 | 2 | 3 | 4 | 5 | 6 | 7 |
|---|---|---|---|---|---|---|---|---|
|  | Reps |  |  |  |  |  |  |  |
|  | Weight |  |  |  |  |  |  |  |
|  | Reps |  |  |  |  |  |  |  |
|  | Weight |  |  |  |  |  |  |  |
|  | Reps |  |  |  |  |  |  |  |
|  | Weight |  |  |  |  |  |  |  |
|  | Reps |  |  |  |  |  |  |  |
|  | Weight |  |  |  |  |  |  |  |
|  | Reps |  |  |  |  |  |  |  |
|  | Weight |  |  |  |  |  |  |  |
|  | Reps |  |  |  |  |  |  |  |
|  | Weight |  |  |  |  |  |  |  |
|  | Reps |  |  |  |  |  |  |  |
|  | Weight |  |  |  |  |  |  |  |
|  | Reps |  |  |  |  |  |  |  |
|  | Weight |  |  |  |  |  |  |  |

| Cardio | Time | Distance | Heart Rate | Cals Burned |
|---|---|---|---|---|
|  |  |  |  |  |
|  |  |  |  |  |
|  |  |  |  |  |

### Measurements

| Neck | R Bicep | L Bicep | Chest | Waist | Hips | R Thigh | L Thigh | Calf |
|---|---|---|---|---|---|---|---|---|
|  |  |  |  |  |  |  |  |  |
|  |  |  |  |  |  |  |  |  |
|  |  |  |  |  |  |  |  |  |

**Date:** _____ **Muscle Group:** _____

S  M  T  W  T  F  S  **Start Time** _____
○  ○  ○  ○  ○  ○  ○

**Weight:** _____ **Finish Time** _____

☐ **Upper Body**　　☐ **Lower Body**　　☐ **Abs**

| Exercise | Set | 1 | 2 | 3 | 4 | 5 | 6 | 7 |
|---|---|---|---|---|---|---|---|---|
|  | Reps |  |  |  |  |  |  |  |
|  | Weight |  |  |  |  |  |  |  |
|  | Reps |  |  |  |  |  |  |  |
|  | Weight |  |  |  |  |  |  |  |
|  | Reps |  |  |  |  |  |  |  |
|  | Weight |  |  |  |  |  |  |  |
|  | Reps |  |  |  |  |  |  |  |
|  | Weight |  |  |  |  |  |  |  |
|  | Reps |  |  |  |  |  |  |  |
|  | Weight |  |  |  |  |  |  |  |
|  | Reps |  |  |  |  |  |  |  |
|  | Weight |  |  |  |  |  |  |  |
|  | Reps |  |  |  |  |  |  |  |
|  | Weight |  |  |  |  |  |  |  |
|  | Reps |  |  |  |  |  |  |  |
|  | Weight |  |  |  |  |  |  |  |

| Cardio | Time | Distance | Heart Rate | Cals Burned |
|---|---|---|---|---|
|  |  |  |  |  |
|  |  |  |  |  |
|  |  |  |  |  |

## Measurements

| Neck | R Bicep | L Bicep | Chest | Waist | Hips | R Thigh | L Thigh | Calf |
|---|---|---|---|---|---|---|---|---|
|  |  |  |  |  |  |  |  |  |
|  |  |  |  |  |  |  |  |  |
|  |  |  |  |  |  |  |  |  |

Date: _____  Muscle Group: _____

S M T W T F S  Start Time _____
○ ○ ○ ○ ○ ○ ○

Weight: _____  Finish Time _____

☐ Upper Body    ☐ Lower Body    ☐ Abs

| Exercise | Set | 1 | 2 | 3 | 4 | 5 | 6 | 7 |
|---|---|---|---|---|---|---|---|---|
|  | Reps |  |  |  |  |  |  |  |
|  | Weight |  |  |  |  |  |  |  |
|  | Reps |  |  |  |  |  |  |  |
|  | Weight |  |  |  |  |  |  |  |
|  | Reps |  |  |  |  |  |  |  |
|  | Weight |  |  |  |  |  |  |  |
|  | Reps |  |  |  |  |  |  |  |
|  | Weight |  |  |  |  |  |  |  |
|  | Reps |  |  |  |  |  |  |  |
|  | Weight |  |  |  |  |  |  |  |
|  | Reps |  |  |  |  |  |  |  |
|  | Weight |  |  |  |  |  |  |  |
|  | Reps |  |  |  |  |  |  |  |
|  | Weight |  |  |  |  |  |  |  |
|  | Reps |  |  |  |  |  |  |  |
|  | Weight |  |  |  |  |  |  |  |

| Cardio | Time | Distance | Heart Rate | Cals Burned |
|---|---|---|---|---|
|  |  |  |  |  |
|  |  |  |  |  |
|  |  |  |  |  |

### Measurements

| Neck | R Bicep | L Bicep | Chest | Waist | Hips | R Thigh | L Thigh | Calf |
|---|---|---|---|---|---|---|---|---|
|  |  |  |  |  |  |  |  |  |
|  |  |  |  |  |  |  |  |  |
|  |  |  |  |  |  |  |  |  |

**Date:**_____   **Muscle Group:** _____

S  M  T  W  T  F  S   **Start Time**_____
○  ○  ○  ○  ○  ○  ○

**Weight:**_____   **Finish Time**_____

☐ Upper Body     ☐ Lower Body     ☐ Abs

| Exercise | Set | 1 | 2 | 3 | 4 | 5 | 6 | 7 |
|---|---|---|---|---|---|---|---|---|
|  | Reps |  |  |  |  |  |  |  |
|  | Weight |  |  |  |  |  |  |  |
|  | Reps |  |  |  |  |  |  |  |
|  | Weight |  |  |  |  |  |  |  |
|  | Reps |  |  |  |  |  |  |  |
|  | Weight |  |  |  |  |  |  |  |
|  | Reps |  |  |  |  |  |  |  |
|  | Weight |  |  |  |  |  |  |  |
|  | Reps |  |  |  |  |  |  |  |
|  | Weight |  |  |  |  |  |  |  |
|  | Reps |  |  |  |  |  |  |  |
|  | Weight |  |  |  |  |  |  |  |
|  | Reps |  |  |  |  |  |  |  |
|  | Weight |  |  |  |  |  |  |  |
|  | Reps |  |  |  |  |  |  |  |
|  | Weight |  |  |  |  |  |  |  |

| Cardio | Time | Distance | Heart Rate | Cals Burned |
|---|---|---|---|---|
|  |  |  |  |  |
|  |  |  |  |  |
|  |  |  |  |  |

### Measurements

| Neck | R Bicep | L Bicep | Chest | Waist | Hips | R Thigh | L Thigh | Calf |
|---|---|---|---|---|---|---|---|---|
|  |  |  |  |  |  |  |  |  |
|  |  |  |  |  |  |  |  |  |
|  |  |  |  |  |  |  |  |  |

Date:_____    Muscle Group:_____

S  M  T  W  T  F  S    Start Time_____
○  ○  ○  ○  ○  ○  ○

Weight:_____    Finish Time_____

☐ Upper Body    ☐ Lower Body    ☐ Abs

| Exercise | Set | 1 | 2 | 3 | 4 | 5 | 6 | 7 |
|---|---|---|---|---|---|---|---|---|
|  | Reps |  |  |  |  |  |  |  |
|  | Weight |  |  |  |  |  |  |  |
|  | Reps |  |  |  |  |  |  |  |
|  | Weight |  |  |  |  |  |  |  |
|  | Reps |  |  |  |  |  |  |  |
|  | Weight |  |  |  |  |  |  |  |
|  | Reps |  |  |  |  |  |  |  |
|  | Weight |  |  |  |  |  |  |  |
|  | Reps |  |  |  |  |  |  |  |
|  | Weight |  |  |  |  |  |  |  |
|  | Reps |  |  |  |  |  |  |  |
|  | Weight |  |  |  |  |  |  |  |
|  | Reps |  |  |  |  |  |  |  |
|  | Weight |  |  |  |  |  |  |  |
|  | Reps |  |  |  |  |  |  |  |
|  | Weight |  |  |  |  |  |  |  |

| Cardio | Time | Distance | Heart Rate | Cals Burned |
|---|---|---|---|---|
|  |  |  |  |  |
|  |  |  |  |  |
|  |  |  |  |  |

## Measurements

| Neck | R Bicep | L Bicep | Chest | Waist | Hips | R Thigh | L Thigh | Calf |
|---|---|---|---|---|---|---|---|---|
|  |  |  |  |  |  |  |  |  |
|  |  |  |  |  |  |  |  |  |
|  |  |  |  |  |  |  |  |  |

**Date:** _____  **Muscle Group:** _____

S M T W T F S  **Start Time** _____
○ ○ ○ ○ ○ ○ ○

**Weight:** _____  **Finish Time** _____

☐ Upper Body    ☐ Lower Body    ☐ Abs

| Exercise | Set | 1 | 2 | 3 | 4 | 5 | 6 | 7 |
|---|---|---|---|---|---|---|---|---|
|  | Reps |  |  |  |  |  |  |  |
|  | Weight |  |  |  |  |  |  |  |
|  | Reps |  |  |  |  |  |  |  |
|  | Weight |  |  |  |  |  |  |  |
|  | Reps |  |  |  |  |  |  |  |
|  | Weight |  |  |  |  |  |  |  |
|  | Reps |  |  |  |  |  |  |  |
|  | Weight |  |  |  |  |  |  |  |
|  | Reps |  |  |  |  |  |  |  |
|  | Weight |  |  |  |  |  |  |  |
|  | Reps |  |  |  |  |  |  |  |
|  | Weight |  |  |  |  |  |  |  |
|  | Reps |  |  |  |  |  |  |  |
|  | Weight |  |  |  |  |  |  |  |
|  | Reps |  |  |  |  |  |  |  |
|  | Weight |  |  |  |  |  |  |  |

| Cardio | Time | Distance | Heart Rate | Cals Burned |
|---|---|---|---|---|
|  |  |  |  |  |
|  |  |  |  |  |
|  |  |  |  |  |

### Measurements

| Neck | R Bicep | L Bicep | Chest | Waist | Hips | R Thigh | L Thigh | Calf |
|---|---|---|---|---|---|---|---|---|
|  |  |  |  |  |  |  |  |  |
|  |  |  |  |  |  |  |  |  |
|  |  |  |  |  |  |  |  |  |

**Date:** _____  **Muscle Group:** _____

S  M  T  W  T  F  S   **Start Time** _____
◯  ◯  ◯  ◯  ◯  ◯  ◯

**Weight:** _____  **Finish Time** _____

☐ Upper Body    ☐ Lower Body    ☐ Abs

| Exercise | Set | 1 | 2 | 3 | 4 | 5 | 6 | 7 |
|---|---|---|---|---|---|---|---|---|
|  | Reps |  |  |  |  |  |  |  |
|  | Weight |  |  |  |  |  |  |  |
|  | Reps |  |  |  |  |  |  |  |
|  | Weight |  |  |  |  |  |  |  |
|  | Reps |  |  |  |  |  |  |  |
|  | Weight |  |  |  |  |  |  |  |
|  | Reps |  |  |  |  |  |  |  |
|  | Weight |  |  |  |  |  |  |  |
|  | Reps |  |  |  |  |  |  |  |
|  | Weight |  |  |  |  |  |  |  |
|  | Reps |  |  |  |  |  |  |  |
|  | Weight |  |  |  |  |  |  |  |
|  | Reps |  |  |  |  |  |  |  |
|  | Weight |  |  |  |  |  |  |  |
|  | Reps |  |  |  |  |  |  |  |
|  | Weight |  |  |  |  |  |  |  |

| Cardio | Time | Distance | Heart Rate | Cals Burned |
|---|---|---|---|---|
|  |  |  |  |  |
|  |  |  |  |  |
|  |  |  |  |  |

## Measurements

| Neck | R Bicep | L Bicep | Chest | Waist | Hips | R Thigh | L Thigh | Calf |
|---|---|---|---|---|---|---|---|---|
|  |  |  |  |  |  |  |  |  |
|  |  |  |  |  |  |  |  |  |
|  |  |  |  |  |  |  |  |  |

**Date:** _____  **Muscle Group:** _____

S  M  T  W  T  F  S
○  ○  ○  ○  ○  ○  ○

**Start Time** _____

**Weight:** _____  **Finish Time** _____

☐ Upper Body    ☐ Lower Body    ☐ Abs

| Exercise | Set | 1 | 2 | 3 | 4 | 5 | 6 | 7 |
|---|---|---|---|---|---|---|---|---|
| | Reps | | | | | | | |
| | Weight | | | | | | | |
| | Reps | | | | | | | |
| | Weight | | | | | | | |
| | Reps | | | | | | | |
| | Weight | | | | | | | |
| | Reps | | | | | | | |
| | Weight | | | | | | | |
| | Reps | | | | | | | |
| | Weight | | | | | | | |
| | Reps | | | | | | | |
| | Weight | | | | | | | |
| | Reps | | | | | | | |
| | Weight | | | | | | | |
| | Reps | | | | | | | |
| | Weight | | | | | | | |

| Cardio | Time | Distance | Heart Rate | Cals Burned |
|---|---|---|---|---|
| | | | | |
| | | | | |
| | | | | |

### Measurements

| Neck | R Bicep | L Bicep | Chest | Waist | Hips | R Thigh | L Thigh | Calf |
|---|---|---|---|---|---|---|---|---|
| | | | | | | | | |
| | | | | | | | | |
| | | | | | | | | |

**Date:** _____  **Muscle Group:** _____

S M T W T F S  **Start Time** _____
○ ○ ○ ○ ○ ○ ○

**Weight:** _____  **Finish Time** _____

☐ Upper Body   ☐ Lower Body   ☐ Abs

| Exercise | Set | 1 | 2 | 3 | 4 | 5 | 6 | 7 |
|---|---|---|---|---|---|---|---|---|
|  | Reps |  |  |  |  |  |  |  |
|  | Weight |  |  |  |  |  |  |  |
|  | Reps |  |  |  |  |  |  |  |
|  | Weight |  |  |  |  |  |  |  |
|  | Reps |  |  |  |  |  |  |  |
|  | Weight |  |  |  |  |  |  |  |
|  | Reps |  |  |  |  |  |  |  |
|  | Weight |  |  |  |  |  |  |  |
|  | Reps |  |  |  |  |  |  |  |
|  | Weight |  |  |  |  |  |  |  |
|  | Reps |  |  |  |  |  |  |  |
|  | Weight |  |  |  |  |  |  |  |
|  | Reps |  |  |  |  |  |  |  |
|  | Weight |  |  |  |  |  |  |  |
|  | Reps |  |  |  |  |  |  |  |
|  | Weight |  |  |  |  |  |  |  |

| Cardio | Time | Distance | Heart Rate | Cals Burned |
|---|---|---|---|---|
|  |  |  |  |  |
|  |  |  |  |  |
|  |  |  |  |  |

### Measurements

| Neck | R Bicep | L Bicep | Chest | Waist | Hips | R Thigh | L Thigh | Calf |
|---|---|---|---|---|---|---|---|---|
|  |  |  |  |  |  |  |  |  |
|  |  |  |  |  |  |  |  |  |
|  |  |  |  |  |  |  |  |  |

**Date:** _____     **Muscle Group:** _____

S  M  T  W  T  F  S      **Start Time** _____
◯  ◯  ◯  ◯  ◯  ◯  ◯

**Weight:** _____     **Finish Time** _____

☐ Upper Body          ☐ Lower Body                    ☐ Abs

| Exercise | Set | 1 | 2 | 3 | 4 | 5 | 6 | 7 |
|---|---|---|---|---|---|---|---|---|
|  | Reps |  |  |  |  |  |  |  |
|  | Weight |  |  |  |  |  |  |  |
|  | Reps |  |  |  |  |  |  |  |
|  | Weight |  |  |  |  |  |  |  |
|  | Reps |  |  |  |  |  |  |  |
|  | Weight |  |  |  |  |  |  |  |
|  | Reps |  |  |  |  |  |  |  |
|  | Weight |  |  |  |  |  |  |  |
|  | Reps |  |  |  |  |  |  |  |
|  | Weight |  |  |  |  |  |  |  |
|  | Reps |  |  |  |  |  |  |  |
|  | Weight |  |  |  |  |  |  |  |
|  | Reps |  |  |  |  |  |  |  |
|  | Weight |  |  |  |  |  |  |  |
|  | Reps |  |  |  |  |  |  |  |
|  | Weight |  |  |  |  |  |  |  |

| Cardio | Time | Distance | Heart Rate | Cals Burned |
|---|---|---|---|---|
|  |  |  |  |  |
|  |  |  |  |  |
|  |  |  |  |  |

### Measurements

| Neck | R Bicep | L Bicep | Chest | Waist | Hips | R Thigh | L Thigh | Calf |
|---|---|---|---|---|---|---|---|---|
|  |  |  |  |  |  |  |  |  |
|  |  |  |  |  |  |  |  |  |
|  |  |  |  |  |  |  |  |  |

Date: _____    Muscle Group: _____

S  M  T  W  T  F  S    Start Time _____
○  ○  ○  ○  ○  ○  ○

Weight: _____    Finish Time _____

☐ Upper Body        ☐ Lower Body        ☐ Abs

| Exercise | Set | 1 | 2 | 3 | 4 | 5 | 6 | 7 |
|---|---|---|---|---|---|---|---|---|
|  | Reps |  |  |  |  |  |  |  |
|  | Weight |  |  |  |  |  |  |  |
|  | Reps |  |  |  |  |  |  |  |
|  | Weight |  |  |  |  |  |  |  |
|  | Reps |  |  |  |  |  |  |  |
|  | Weight |  |  |  |  |  |  |  |
|  | Reps |  |  |  |  |  |  |  |
|  | Weight |  |  |  |  |  |  |  |
|  | Reps |  |  |  |  |  |  |  |
|  | Weight |  |  |  |  |  |  |  |
|  | Reps |  |  |  |  |  |  |  |
|  | Weight |  |  |  |  |  |  |  |
|  | Reps |  |  |  |  |  |  |  |
|  | Weight |  |  |  |  |  |  |  |
|  | Reps |  |  |  |  |  |  |  |
|  | Weight |  |  |  |  |  |  |  |

| Cardio | Time | Distance | Heart Rate | Cals Burned |
|---|---|---|---|---|
|  |  |  |  |  |
|  |  |  |  |  |
|  |  |  |  |  |

## Measurements

| Neck | R Bicep | L Bicep | Chest | Waist | Hips | R Thigh | L Thigh | Calf |
|---|---|---|---|---|---|---|---|---|
|  |  |  |  |  |  |  |  |  |
|  |  |  |  |  |  |  |  |  |
|  |  |  |  |  |  |  |  |  |

**Date:** _____  **Muscle Group:** _____

S  M  T  W  T  F  S  **Start Time** _____
○  ○  ○  ○  ○  ○  ○

**Weight:** _____  **Finish Time** _____

☐ Upper Body    ☐ Lower Body    ☐ Abs

| Exercise | Set | 1 | 2 | 3 | 4 | 5 | 6 | 7 |
|---|---|---|---|---|---|---|---|---|
|  | Reps |  |  |  |  |  |  |  |
|  | Weight |  |  |  |  |  |  |  |
|  | Reps |  |  |  |  |  |  |  |
|  | Weight |  |  |  |  |  |  |  |
|  | Reps |  |  |  |  |  |  |  |
|  | Weight |  |  |  |  |  |  |  |
|  | Reps |  |  |  |  |  |  |  |
|  | Weight |  |  |  |  |  |  |  |
|  | Reps |  |  |  |  |  |  |  |
|  | Weight |  |  |  |  |  |  |  |
|  | Reps |  |  |  |  |  |  |  |
|  | Weight |  |  |  |  |  |  |  |
|  | Reps |  |  |  |  |  |  |  |
|  | Weight |  |  |  |  |  |  |  |
|  | Reps |  |  |  |  |  |  |  |
|  | Weight |  |  |  |  |  |  |  |

| Cardio | Time | Distance | Heart Rate | Cals Burned |
|---|---|---|---|---|
|  |  |  |  |  |
|  |  |  |  |  |
|  |  |  |  |  |

## Measurements

| Neck | R Bicep | L Bicep | Chest | Waist | Hips | R Thigh | L Thigh | Calf |
|---|---|---|---|---|---|---|---|---|
|  |  |  |  |  |  |  |  |  |
|  |  |  |  |  |  |  |  |  |
|  |  |  |  |  |  |  |  |  |

**Date:** _____  **Muscle Group:** _____

S  M  T  W  T  F  S
◯  ◯  ◯  ◯  ◯  ◯  ◯   **Start Time** _____

**Weight:** _____   **Finish Time** _____

☐ Upper Body     ☐ Lower Body     ☐ Abs

| Exercise | Set | 1 | 2 | 3 | 4 | 5 | 6 | 7 |
|---|---|---|---|---|---|---|---|---|
|  | Reps |  |  |  |  |  |  |  |
|  | Weight |  |  |  |  |  |  |  |
|  | Reps |  |  |  |  |  |  |  |
|  | Weight |  |  |  |  |  |  |  |
|  | Reps |  |  |  |  |  |  |  |
|  | Weight |  |  |  |  |  |  |  |
|  | Reps |  |  |  |  |  |  |  |
|  | Weight |  |  |  |  |  |  |  |
|  | Reps |  |  |  |  |  |  |  |
|  | Weight |  |  |  |  |  |  |  |
|  | Reps |  |  |  |  |  |  |  |
|  | Weight |  |  |  |  |  |  |  |
|  | Reps |  |  |  |  |  |  |  |
|  | Weight |  |  |  |  |  |  |  |
|  | Reps |  |  |  |  |  |  |  |
|  | Weight |  |  |  |  |  |  |  |

| Cardio | Time | Distance | Heart Rate | Cals Burned |
|---|---|---|---|---|
|  |  |  |  |  |
|  |  |  |  |  |
|  |  |  |  |  |

### Measurements

| Neck | R Bicep | L Bicep | Chest | Waist | Hips | R Thigh | L Thigh | Calf |
|---|---|---|---|---|---|---|---|---|
|  |  |  |  |  |  |  |  |  |
|  |  |  |  |  |  |  |  |  |
|  |  |  |  |  |  |  |  |  |

**Date:** _____  **Muscle Group:** _____

S  M  T  W  T  F  S   **Start Time** _____
◯  ◯  ◯  ◯  ◯  ◯  ◯

**Weight:** _____  **Finish Time** _____

☐ **Upper Body**   ☐ **Lower Body**   ☐ **Abs**

| Exercise | Set | 1 | 2 | 3 | 4 | 5 | 6 | 7 |
|---|---|---|---|---|---|---|---|---|
|  | Reps |  |  |  |  |  |  |  |
|  | Weight |  |  |  |  |  |  |  |
|  | Reps |  |  |  |  |  |  |  |
|  | Weight |  |  |  |  |  |  |  |
|  | Reps |  |  |  |  |  |  |  |
|  | Weight |  |  |  |  |  |  |  |
|  | Reps |  |  |  |  |  |  |  |
|  | Weight |  |  |  |  |  |  |  |
|  | Reps |  |  |  |  |  |  |  |
|  | Weight |  |  |  |  |  |  |  |
|  | Reps |  |  |  |  |  |  |  |
|  | Weight |  |  |  |  |  |  |  |
|  | Reps |  |  |  |  |  |  |  |
|  | Weight |  |  |  |  |  |  |  |
|  | Reps |  |  |  |  |  |  |  |
|  | Weight |  |  |  |  |  |  |  |

| Cardio | Time | Distance | Heart Rate | Cals Burned |
|---|---|---|---|---|
|  |  |  |  |  |
|  |  |  |  |  |
|  |  |  |  |  |

### Measurements

| Neck | R Bicep | L Bicep | Chest | Waist | Hips | R Thigh | L Thigh | Calf |
|---|---|---|---|---|---|---|---|---|
|  |  |  |  |  |  |  |  |  |
|  |  |  |  |  |  |  |  |  |
|  |  |  |  |  |  |  |  |  |

**Date:** _____  **Muscle Group:** _____

S M T W T F S  **Start Time** _____
○ ○ ○ ○ ○ ○ ○

**Weight:** _____  **Finish Time** _____

☐ Upper Body   ☐ Lower Body   ☐ Abs

| Exercise | Set | 1 | 2 | 3 | 4 | 5 | 6 | 7 |
|---|---|---|---|---|---|---|---|---|
| | Reps | | | | | | | |
| | Weight | | | | | | | |
| | Reps | | | | | | | |
| | Weight | | | | | | | |
| | Reps | | | | | | | |
| | Weight | | | | | | | |
| | Reps | | | | | | | |
| | Weight | | | | | | | |
| | Reps | | | | | | | |
| | Weight | | | | | | | |
| | Reps | | | | | | | |
| | Weight | | | | | | | |
| | Reps | | | | | | | |
| | Weight | | | | | | | |
| | Reps | | | | | | | |
| | Weight | | | | | | | |

| Cardio | Time | Distance | Heart Rate | Cals Burned |
|---|---|---|---|---|
| | | | | |
| | | | | |
| | | | | |

### Measurements

| Neck | R Bicep | L Bicep | Chest | Waist | Hips | R Thigh | L Thigh | Calf |
|---|---|---|---|---|---|---|---|---|
| | | | | | | | | |
| | | | | | | | | |
| | | | | | | | | |

**Date:** _____  **Muscle Group:** _____

S  M  T  W  T  F  S    **Start Time** _____
○  ○  ○  ○  ○  ○  ○

**Weight:** _____   **Finish Time** _____

☐ **Upper Body**    ☐ **Lower Body**    ☐ **Abs**

| Exercise | Set | 1 | 2 | 3 | 4 | 5 | 6 | 7 |
|---|---|---|---|---|---|---|---|---|
|  | Reps |  |  |  |  |  |  |  |
|  | Weight |  |  |  |  |  |  |  |
|  | Reps |  |  |  |  |  |  |  |
|  | Weight |  |  |  |  |  |  |  |
|  | Reps |  |  |  |  |  |  |  |
|  | Weight |  |  |  |  |  |  |  |
|  | Reps |  |  |  |  |  |  |  |
|  | Weight |  |  |  |  |  |  |  |
|  | Reps |  |  |  |  |  |  |  |
|  | Weight |  |  |  |  |  |  |  |
|  | Reps |  |  |  |  |  |  |  |
|  | Weight |  |  |  |  |  |  |  |
|  | Reps |  |  |  |  |  |  |  |
|  | Weight |  |  |  |  |  |  |  |
|  | Reps |  |  |  |  |  |  |  |
|  | Weight |  |  |  |  |  |  |  |

| Cardio | Time | Distance | Heart Rate | Cals Burned |
|---|---|---|---|---|
|  |  |  |  |  |
|  |  |  |  |  |
|  |  |  |  |  |

## Measurements

| Neck | R Bicep | L Bicep | Chest | Waist | Hips | R Thigh | L Thigh | Calf |
|---|---|---|---|---|---|---|---|---|
|  |  |  |  |  |  |  |  |  |
|  |  |  |  |  |  |  |  |  |
|  |  |  |  |  |  |  |  |  |

Date:_____ Muscle Group: _____

S M T W T F S  Start Time_____
○ ○ ○ ○ ○ ○ ○

Weight:_____ Finish Time_____

☐ Upper Body   ☐ Lower Body   ☐ Abs

| Exercise | Set | 1 | 2 | 3 | 4 | 5 | 6 | 7 |
|---|---|---|---|---|---|---|---|---|
|  | Reps |  |  |  |  |  |  |  |
|  | Weight |  |  |  |  |  |  |  |
|  | Reps |  |  |  |  |  |  |  |
|  | Weight |  |  |  |  |  |  |  |
|  | Reps |  |  |  |  |  |  |  |
|  | Weight |  |  |  |  |  |  |  |
|  | Reps |  |  |  |  |  |  |  |
|  | Weight |  |  |  |  |  |  |  |
|  | Reps |  |  |  |  |  |  |  |
|  | Weight |  |  |  |  |  |  |  |
|  | Reps |  |  |  |  |  |  |  |
|  | Weight |  |  |  |  |  |  |  |
|  | Reps |  |  |  |  |  |  |  |
|  | Weight |  |  |  |  |  |  |  |
|  | Reps |  |  |  |  |  |  |  |
|  | Weight |  |  |  |  |  |  |  |

| Cardio | Time | Distance | Heart Rate | Cals Burned |
|---|---|---|---|---|
|  |  |  |  |  |
|  |  |  |  |  |
|  |  |  |  |  |

## Measurements

| Neck | R Bicep | L Bicep | Chest | Waist | Hips | R Thigh | L Thigh | Calf |
|---|---|---|---|---|---|---|---|---|
|  |  |  |  |  |  |  |  |  |
|  |  |  |  |  |  |  |  |  |
|  |  |  |  |  |  |  |  |  |

**Date:** _____ **Muscle Group:** _____

S  M  T  W  T  F  S   **Start Time** _____
○  ○  ○  ○  ○  ○  ○

**Weight:** _____ **Finish Time** _____

☐ **Upper Body**   ☐ **Lower Body**   ☐ **Abs**

| Exercise | Set | 1 | 2 | 3 | 4 | 5 | 6 | 7 |
|---|---|---|---|---|---|---|---|---|
|  | Reps |  |  |  |  |  |  |  |
|  | Weight |  |  |  |  |  |  |  |
|  | Reps |  |  |  |  |  |  |  |
|  | Weight |  |  |  |  |  |  |  |
|  | Reps |  |  |  |  |  |  |  |
|  | Weight |  |  |  |  |  |  |  |
|  | Reps |  |  |  |  |  |  |  |
|  | Weight |  |  |  |  |  |  |  |
|  | Reps |  |  |  |  |  |  |  |
|  | Weight |  |  |  |  |  |  |  |
|  | Reps |  |  |  |  |  |  |  |
|  | Weight |  |  |  |  |  |  |  |
|  | Reps |  |  |  |  |  |  |  |
|  | Weight |  |  |  |  |  |  |  |
|  | Reps |  |  |  |  |  |  |  |
|  | Weight |  |  |  |  |  |  |  |

| Cardio | Time | Distance | Heart Rate | Cals Burned |
|---|---|---|---|---|
|  |  |  |  |  |
|  |  |  |  |  |
|  |  |  |  |  |

## Measurements

| Neck | R Bicep | L Bicep | Chest | Waist | Hips | R Thigh | L Thigh | Calf |
|---|---|---|---|---|---|---|---|---|
|  |  |  |  |  |  |  |  |  |
|  |  |  |  |  |  |  |  |  |
|  |  |  |  |  |  |  |  |  |

**Date:** _____  **Muscle Group:** _____

S M T W T F S  **Start Time** _____
◯ ◯ ◯ ◯ ◯ ◯ ◯

**Weight:** _____  **Finish Time** _____

☐ Upper Body    ☐ Lower Body    ☐ Abs

| Exercise | Set | 1 | 2 | 3 | 4 | 5 | 6 | 7 |
|---|---|---|---|---|---|---|---|---|
|  | Reps |  |  |  |  |  |  |  |
|  | Weight |  |  |  |  |  |  |  |
|  | Reps |  |  |  |  |  |  |  |
|  | Weight |  |  |  |  |  |  |  |
|  | Reps |  |  |  |  |  |  |  |
|  | Weight |  |  |  |  |  |  |  |
|  | Reps |  |  |  |  |  |  |  |
|  | Weight |  |  |  |  |  |  |  |
|  | Reps |  |  |  |  |  |  |  |
|  | Weight |  |  |  |  |  |  |  |
|  | Reps |  |  |  |  |  |  |  |
|  | Weight |  |  |  |  |  |  |  |
|  | Reps |  |  |  |  |  |  |  |
|  | Weight |  |  |  |  |  |  |  |
|  | Reps |  |  |  |  |  |  |  |
|  | Weight |  |  |  |  |  |  |  |

| Cardio | Time | Distance | Heart Rate | Cals Burned |
|---|---|---|---|---|
|  |  |  |  |  |
|  |  |  |  |  |
|  |  |  |  |  |

## Measurements

| Neck | R Bicep | L Bicep | Chest | Waist | Hips | R Thigh | L Thigh | Calf |
|---|---|---|---|---|---|---|---|---|
|  |  |  |  |  |  |  |  |  |
|  |  |  |  |  |  |  |  |  |
|  |  |  |  |  |  |  |  |  |

**Date:** _____  **Muscle Group:** _____

S  M  T  W  T  F  S   **Start Time** _____
◯  ◯  ◯  ◯  ◯  ◯  ◯

**Weight:** _____  **Finish Time** _____

☐ Upper Body   ☐ Lower Body   ☐ Abs

| Exercise | Set | 1 | 2 | 3 | 4 | 5 | 6 | 7 |
|---|---|---|---|---|---|---|---|---|
| | Reps | | | | | | | |
| | Weight | | | | | | | |
| | Reps | | | | | | | |
| | Weight | | | | | | | |
| | Reps | | | | | | | |
| | Weight | | | | | | | |
| | Reps | | | | | | | |
| | Weight | | | | | | | |
| | Reps | | | | | | | |
| | Weight | | | | | | | |
| | Reps | | | | | | | |
| | Weight | | | | | | | |
| | Reps | | | | | | | |
| | Weight | | | | | | | |
| | Reps | | | | | | | |
| | Weight | | | | | | | |

| Cardio | Time | Distance | Heart Rate | Cals Burned |
|---|---|---|---|---|
| | | | | |
| | | | | |
| | | | | |

## Measurements

| Neck | R Bicep | L Bicep | Chest | Waist | Hips | R Thigh | L Thigh | Calf |
|---|---|---|---|---|---|---|---|---|
| | | | | | | | | |
| | | | | | | | | |
| | | | | | | | | |

**Date:**_____  **Muscle Group:** _____

S  M  T  W  T  F  S    **Start Time**_____
○  ○  ○  ○  ○  ○  ○

**Weight:**_____  **Finish Time**_____

☐ Upper Body    ☐ Lower Body    ☐ Abs

| Exercise | Set | 1 | 2 | 3 | 4 | 5 | 6 | 7 |
|---|---|---|---|---|---|---|---|---|
|  | Reps |  |  |  |  |  |  |  |
|  | Weight |  |  |  |  |  |  |  |
|  | Reps |  |  |  |  |  |  |  |
|  | Weight |  |  |  |  |  |  |  |
|  | Reps |  |  |  |  |  |  |  |
|  | Weight |  |  |  |  |  |  |  |
|  | Reps |  |  |  |  |  |  |  |
|  | Weight |  |  |  |  |  |  |  |
|  | Reps |  |  |  |  |  |  |  |
|  | Weight |  |  |  |  |  |  |  |
|  | Reps |  |  |  |  |  |  |  |
|  | Weight |  |  |  |  |  |  |  |
|  | Reps |  |  |  |  |  |  |  |
|  | Weight |  |  |  |  |  |  |  |
|  | Reps |  |  |  |  |  |  |  |
|  | Weight |  |  |  |  |  |  |  |

| Cardio | Time | Distance | Heart Rate | Cals Burned |
|---|---|---|---|---|
|  |  |  |  |  |
|  |  |  |  |  |
|  |  |  |  |  |

### Measurements

| Neck | R Bicep | L Bicep | Chest | Waist | Hips | R Thigh | L Thigh | Calf |
|---|---|---|---|---|---|---|---|---|
|  |  |  |  |  |  |  |  |  |
|  |  |  |  |  |  |  |  |  |
|  |  |  |  |  |  |  |  |  |

**Date:** _____   **Muscle Group:** _____

S  M  T  W  T  F  S   **Start Time** _____
◯ ◯ ◯ ◯ ◯ ◯ ◯

**Weight:** _____   **Finish Time** _____

☐ Upper Body   ☐ Lower Body   ☐ Abs

| Exercise | Set | 1 | 2 | 3 | 4 | 5 | 6 | 7 |
|---|---|---|---|---|---|---|---|---|
|  | Reps |  |  |  |  |  |  |  |
|  | Weight |  |  |  |  |  |  |  |
|  | Reps |  |  |  |  |  |  |  |
|  | Weight |  |  |  |  |  |  |  |
|  | Reps |  |  |  |  |  |  |  |
|  | Weight |  |  |  |  |  |  |  |
|  | Reps |  |  |  |  |  |  |  |
|  | Weight |  |  |  |  |  |  |  |
|  | Reps |  |  |  |  |  |  |  |
|  | Weight |  |  |  |  |  |  |  |
|  | Reps |  |  |  |  |  |  |  |
|  | Weight |  |  |  |  |  |  |  |
|  | Reps |  |  |  |  |  |  |  |
|  | Weight |  |  |  |  |  |  |  |
|  | Reps |  |  |  |  |  |  |  |
|  | Weight |  |  |  |  |  |  |  |

| Cardio | Time | Distance | Heart Rate | Cals Burned |
|---|---|---|---|---|
|  |  |  |  |  |
|  |  |  |  |  |
|  |  |  |  |  |

## Measurements

| Neck | R Bicep | L Bicep | Chest | Waist | Hips | R Thigh | L Thigh | Calf |
|---|---|---|---|---|---|---|---|---|
|  |  |  |  |  |  |  |  |  |
|  |  |  |  |  |  |  |  |  |
|  |  |  |  |  |  |  |  |  |

Date: _____  Muscle Group: _____

S M T W T F S  Start Time _____
○ ○ ○ ○ ○ ○ ○

Weight: _____  Finish Time _____

☐ Upper Body    ☐ Lower Body    ☐ Abs

| Exercise | Set | 1 | 2 | 3 | 4 | 5 | 6 | 7 |
|---|---|---|---|---|---|---|---|---|
|  | Reps |  |  |  |  |  |  |  |
|  | Weight |  |  |  |  |  |  |  |
|  | Reps |  |  |  |  |  |  |  |
|  | Weight |  |  |  |  |  |  |  |
|  | Reps |  |  |  |  |  |  |  |
|  | Weight |  |  |  |  |  |  |  |
|  | Reps |  |  |  |  |  |  |  |
|  | Weight |  |  |  |  |  |  |  |
|  | Reps |  |  |  |  |  |  |  |
|  | Weight |  |  |  |  |  |  |  |
|  | Reps |  |  |  |  |  |  |  |
|  | Weight |  |  |  |  |  |  |  |
|  | Reps |  |  |  |  |  |  |  |
|  | Weight |  |  |  |  |  |  |  |
|  | Reps |  |  |  |  |  |  |  |
|  | Weight |  |  |  |  |  |  |  |

| Cardio | Time | Distance | Heart Rate | Cals Burned |
|---|---|---|---|---|
|  |  |  |  |  |
|  |  |  |  |  |
|  |  |  |  |  |

## Measurements

| Neck | R Bicep | L Bicep | Chest | Waist | Hips | R Thigh | L Thigh | Calf |
|---|---|---|---|---|---|---|---|---|
|  |  |  |  |  |  |  |  |  |
|  |  |  |  |  |  |  |  |  |
|  |  |  |  |  |  |  |  |  |

**Date:** _____  **Muscle Group:** _____

S  M  T  W  T  F  S  **Start Time** _____
○  ○  ○  ○  ○  ○  ○

**Weight:** _____  **Finish Time** _____

☐ Upper Body   ☐ Lower Body   ☐ Abs

| Exercise | Set | 1 | 2 | 3 | 4 | 5 | 6 | 7 |
|---|---|---|---|---|---|---|---|---|
|  | Reps |  |  |  |  |  |  |  |
|  | Weight |  |  |  |  |  |  |  |
|  | Reps |  |  |  |  |  |  |  |
|  | Weight |  |  |  |  |  |  |  |
|  | Reps |  |  |  |  |  |  |  |
|  | Weight |  |  |  |  |  |  |  |
|  | Reps |  |  |  |  |  |  |  |
|  | Weight |  |  |  |  |  |  |  |
|  | Reps |  |  |  |  |  |  |  |
|  | Weight |  |  |  |  |  |  |  |
|  | Reps |  |  |  |  |  |  |  |
|  | Weight |  |  |  |  |  |  |  |
|  | Reps |  |  |  |  |  |  |  |
|  | Weight |  |  |  |  |  |  |  |
|  | Reps |  |  |  |  |  |  |  |
|  | Weight |  |  |  |  |  |  |  |

| Cardio | Time | Distance | Heart Rate | Cals Burned |
|---|---|---|---|---|
|  |  |  |  |  |
|  |  |  |  |  |
|  |  |  |  |  |

## Measurements

| Neck | R Bicep | L Bicep | Chest | Waist | Hips | R Thigh | L Thigh | Calf |
|---|---|---|---|---|---|---|---|---|
|  |  |  |  |  |  |  |  |  |
|  |  |  |  |  |  |  |  |  |
|  |  |  |  |  |  |  |  |  |

**Date:** _____  **Muscle Group:** _____

S ○  M ○  T ○  W ○  T ○  F ○  S ○    **Start Time** _____

**Weight:** _____  **Finish Time** _____

☐ **Upper Body**  ☐ **Lower Body**  ☐ **Abs**

| Exercise | Set | 1 | 2 | 3 | 4 | 5 | 6 | 7 |
|---|---|---|---|---|---|---|---|---|
|  | Reps |  |  |  |  |  |  |  |
|  | Weight |  |  |  |  |  |  |  |
|  | Reps |  |  |  |  |  |  |  |
|  | Weight |  |  |  |  |  |  |  |
|  | Reps |  |  |  |  |  |  |  |
|  | Weight |  |  |  |  |  |  |  |
|  | Reps |  |  |  |  |  |  |  |
|  | Weight |  |  |  |  |  |  |  |
|  | Reps |  |  |  |  |  |  |  |
|  | Weight |  |  |  |  |  |  |  |
|  | Reps |  |  |  |  |  |  |  |
|  | Weight |  |  |  |  |  |  |  |
|  | Reps |  |  |  |  |  |  |  |
|  | Weight |  |  |  |  |  |  |  |
|  | Reps |  |  |  |  |  |  |  |
|  | Weight |  |  |  |  |  |  |  |

| Cardio | Time | Distance | Heart Rate | Cals Burned |
|---|---|---|---|---|
|  |  |  |  |  |
|  |  |  |  |  |
|  |  |  |  |  |

### Measurements

| Neck | R Bicep | L Bicep | Chest | Waist | Hips | R Thigh | L Thigh | Calf |
|---|---|---|---|---|---|---|---|---|
|  |  |  |  |  |  |  |  |  |
|  |  |  |  |  |  |  |  |  |
|  |  |  |  |  |  |  |  |  |

**Date:** _____  **Muscle Group:** _____

S  M  T  W  T  F  S  **Start Time** _____
○  ○  ○  ○  ○  ○  ○

**Weight:** _____  **Finish Time** _____

☐ Upper Body      ☐ Lower Body      ☐ Abs

| Exercise | Set | 1 | 2 | 3 | 4 | 5 | 6 | 7 |
|---|---|---|---|---|---|---|---|---|
|  | Reps |  |  |  |  |  |  |  |
|  | Weight |  |  |  |  |  |  |  |
|  | Reps |  |  |  |  |  |  |  |
|  | Weight |  |  |  |  |  |  |  |
|  | Reps |  |  |  |  |  |  |  |
|  | Weight |  |  |  |  |  |  |  |
|  | Reps |  |  |  |  |  |  |  |
|  | Weight |  |  |  |  |  |  |  |
|  | Reps |  |  |  |  |  |  |  |
|  | Weight |  |  |  |  |  |  |  |
|  | Reps |  |  |  |  |  |  |  |
|  | Weight |  |  |  |  |  |  |  |
|  | Reps |  |  |  |  |  |  |  |
|  | Weight |  |  |  |  |  |  |  |
|  | Reps |  |  |  |  |  |  |  |
|  | Weight |  |  |  |  |  |  |  |

| Cardio | Time | Distance | Heart Rate | Cals Burned |
|---|---|---|---|---|
|  |  |  |  |  |
|  |  |  |  |  |
|  |  |  |  |  |

### Measurements

| Neck | R Bicep | L Bicep | Chest | Waist | Hips | R Thigh | L Thigh | Calf |
|---|---|---|---|---|---|---|---|---|
|  |  |  |  |  |  |  |  |  |
|  |  |  |  |  |  |  |  |  |
|  |  |  |  |  |  |  |  |  |

# Thank you!

WE ARE GLAD THAT YOU PURCHASED OUR BOOK!
PLEASE LET US KNOW HOW WE CAN IMPROVE IT!
YOUR FEEDBACK IS ESSENTIAL TO US.

Contact us at:

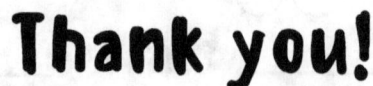 log'Sin@gmail.com

---

JUST TITLE THE EMAIL 'CREATIVE' AND WE WILL GIVE YOU SOME EXTRA SURPRISES!

www.ingramcontent.com/pod-product-compliance
Lightning Source LLC
Chambersburg PA
CBHW050308120526
44590CB00016B/2537